TEDDY ROOSEVELT
IN CALIFORNIA

★

THE WHISTLE STOP TOUR THAT CHANGED AMERICA

CHRIS EPTING

THE
History
PRESS

Published by The History Press
Charleston, SC
www.historypress.net

Images courtesy the author unless otherwise noted.

First published 2015

Manufactured in the United States

ISBN 978.1.62619.801.2

Library of Congress Control Number: 2015948834

This book is dedicated to the Honorable William Alsup, U.S. district judge, and the late Steve Medley (longtime head of the Yosemite Association). Thanks to the passion and dedicated efforts of these two friends, today there is now a place recognized as "Roosevelt Point" located in Yosemite National Park near one of the spots where President Theodore Roosevelt and John Muir camped out in 1903. Judge Alsup continues to wander and explore throughout the Sierras, and I'm deeply grateful to him for sharing his story with me. This dedication also extends to the National Park Service for its terrific resources, remarkable employees and steadfast dedication to protecting, preserving and maintaining places like Yosemite.

CONTENTS

ACKNOWLEDGEMENTS

Speeches and quotes herein came primarily from the Library of Congress and the Theodore Roosevelt Collection at Harvard Library. I'd also like to thank Heather Cole, assistant curator of modern books and manuscripts and curator of the Theodore Roosevelt Collection, Houghton Library, Harvard University, for her support in helping me procure certain photos for this book and for her additional assistance. Thanks also to Bob Webber at the Pullman Library for helping me trace what became of President Roosevelt's personal train car from the historic 1903 tour of western states. Thanks to Lynn Northrop at the Raymond Museum in Raymond, California, for her wonderful knowledge regarding her town's special history and how it relates to the journey. As always, thanks to the team at The History Press, including Megan Laddusaw, Ryan Finn and Anna Burrous, as well as to Jerry Roberts for helping me get this project up and running. Most of all, thank you to my family, for always supporting labors of love like this. And last but not least, thank you, the reader, for your interest. It means more than I can express.

INTRODUCTION

To start, here are a few words from Theodore Roosevelt, a president who truly loved and appreciated nature:

We have fallen heirs to the most glorious heritage a people ever received, and each one must do his part if we wish to show that the nation is worthy of its good fortune.

A grove of giant redwood or sequoias should be kept just as we keep a great and beautiful cathedral.

We have become great because of the lavish use of our resources. But the time has come to inquire seriously what will happen when our forests are gone, when the coal, the iron, the oil, and the gas are exhausted, when the soils have still further impoverished and washed into the streams, polluting the rivers, denuding the fields and obstructing navigation.

I recognize the right and duty of this generation to develop and use the natural resources of our land; but I do not recognize the right to waste them, or to rob, by wasteful use, the generations that come after us.

Of all the questions which can come before this nation, short of the actual preservation of its existence in a great war, there is none which compares in importance with the great central task of leaving this land even a better land for our descendants than it is for us.

Spring would not be spring without bird songs, any more than it would be spring without buds and flowers, and I only wish that besides protecting the songsters, the birds of the grove, the orchard, the garden and the meadow, we could also protect the birds of the sea-shore and of the wilderness.

Life is a great adventure…accept it in such a spirit.

Some historians call Theodore Roosevelt the "father of conservation." As president, he authorized the creation of 150 national forests, 18 national monuments, 5 national parks, 4 national game preserves and 51 federal bird reservations.

In 1903, two years after becoming our nation's youngest president (age forty-two) after the assassination of William McKinley, Roosevelt embarked on his first trip to the West Coast not only to help shore up votes for the following year's election but also to explore and get lost in nature.

The April–June 1903 tour of the West remains one of the most important presidential sojourns in history. Fourteen thousand miles through twenty-five states, nearly 150 towns and cities and more than two hundred speeches (including five major addresses). Those two months away from Washington, D.C., changed Roosevelt for the better, and our country is still feeling the positive impact of the journey. The centerpiece of the trip was Roosevelt's first visit to California, where he would spend nearly three weeks. But squeezed in between the appearances and pageantry was a historic three-day wilderness adventure at Yosemite with naturalist John Muir. That brief camping trip in Yosemite proved to be a game changer for the wide-eyed president who loved the rugged great outdoors and would soon, thanks to Muir, work even harder to protect it.

After the trip, Addison C. Thomas was commissioned to write an account of the trek entitled *Roosevelt Among the People*. Only nine copies of the book were published, with the first copy being presented to Roosevelt himself. Addison's preface began:

Not since the time of Napoleon has there been a man of affairs on the world's stage who has attracted the attention of all nations and classes of people as does Col. Theodore Roosevelt. He is picturesque, aggressive, courageous and honest. The stirring events of the past few weeks, in his triumphal march through Europe on his mission of peace has called renewed attention to these same triumphal marches in the United States, when he went among the people to learn their views and expound his doctrine, while President of the United States.

President Theodore Roosevelt, pictured in 1903.

The most notable of these journeys was in the spring of 1903, when he went from the Atlantic to the Pacific and through the South and Southwest, being received everywhere by the acclaim of the multitude, regardless of political affiliation. The journey, and the speeches which he delivered make a most interesting and thrilling chapter in the history of our country.

INTRODUCTION

No citizen of the Republic can be well informed on public affairs who is not intimately acquainted with the events of this historic trip. The pages of this book have been carefully compiled, so as to cover in a most striking, yet accurate manner, every event of Col. Roosevelt's journey, and so well has this been done that the result has received his personal endorsement.

My mission with this book was to document—using articles, speeches and recollections—Roosevelt's first visit to the Golden State, with a particular focus on his time spent in the woods of Yosemite with John Muir, with whom Roosevelt engaged before the trip as a means of broadening his knowledge of the area while spending time with someone who, by then, had become one of the world's most well-known and respected naturalists.

Chapter 1

A MAN NAMED MUIR

John Muir was born on April 21, 1838, in Dunbar, Scotland. As early as 1876, he urged the federal government to adopt a forest conservation policy through articles published in popular periodicals. After first visiting California's Yosemite Valley in 1868 and taking on work as a shepherd, Muir landed a mill job working with James Mason Hutchings, although the two would later have a falling out. Muir began having his ecology-oriented articles published via newspapers in the early 1870s, with his first printed essay appearing in the *New York Tribune*. After much study, he offered revolutionary theories about Yosemite's geological structures being formed by glacial activity, countering previous scientific assertions. In 1892, he founded the Sierra Club. He served as its first president, a position he held until his death in 1914. He was largely responsible for the establishment of Sequoia and Yosemite National Parks. By 1903, he had become famous as a naturalist, writer and conservation advocate.

John Muir's writings had been followed closely by the president, and over time Roosevelt became increasingly interested in discussing his own attitudes toward conservation with Muir face to face. Through California senator Chester Rowell, he communicated to Muir an interest in meeting with him in Yosemite and away from the main party of dignitaries. The rest, as they say, is history. On March 14, 1903, the following letter was sent to the famed naturalist from the White House:

The naturalist John Muir.

My dear Mr. Muir:

Through the courtesy of President Wheeler I have already been in communication with you, but I wish to write you personally to express the hope that you will be able to take me through the Yosemite. I do not want anyone with me but you, and I want to drop politics absolutely for four days and just be out in the open with you. John Burroughs is probably going through the Yellowstone Park with me, and I want to go with you through the Yosemite.

Sincerely yours,
Theodore Roosevelt

On March 27, 1903, Muir responded:

Dear Mr. Roosevelt:

I sincerely thank you for the honor you do me in hoping I may be able to take you through the Yosemite. An engagement to go abroad with Professor Sargent at first stood in the way; but a few small changes have brought our trip into harmony with yours & of course I shall go with you gladly.

Faithfully yours,
John Muir

And so a plan was set into motion. For nearly forty years, *Yosemite Nature Notes* served the park and the National Park Service's interpretive program. First mimeographed as a newsletter in July 10, 1922, *Nature Notes* evolved into a small monthly booklet containing interesting Yosemite-themed articles. In 1955, an article entitled "Roosevelt and Muir—Conservationists" was written by ranger-naturalist Richard J. Hartesveldt and, as background, appears here in part (the rest follows later in the book):

Their Common Values

In May 1903, Yosemite National Park was host to a meeting between President Theodore Roosevelt and John Muir, the famous naturalist. That this historic meeting happened was little known at the time. This unusual meeting of two great conservationists had a strong influence upon the formulation in our government's land and resources policy. It was during this great era of accomplishments that the term conservation came into its present meaning.

The prelude to this meeting began a few years earlier when forests which had been set aside by Presidents Harrison and Cleveland were endangered by pressure from commercial interests who wanted the Congress to release them from Federal control.

To John Muir, through his vivid writings, goes much of the credit for preventing the passage of such legislation. President McKinley devoted a large portion of his time to the management of the unpopular Spanish American War and too little attention was given to land and resource legislation. Through the political maneuvering of his opponents in New York, Governor Theodore Roosevelt was elevated to the vice-presidency in an effort to stem the rash of anti-monopolistic legislation he was proposing.

Meanwhile, the opponents of Federally owned forests were making headway. In a letter to his friend C.S. Sargent, a renowned tree expert, Muir wrote, "In the excitement and din of this confounded war, the silent trees stand a poor show for justice."

But things changed. On September 6, 1901, President McKinley was assassinated; on the same day Theodore Roosevelt was sworn in as President of the United States.

TEDDY ROOSEVELT THE PERFECT MAN FOR THE JOB

Few men have entered the office of President with more enthusiasm than did Teddy Roosevelt. As an outdoorsman, he had a wonderful insight to problems of land management, many of which were solved during his administration.

He felt that "Conservation of natural resources is the fundamental problem." He continued, "Unless we solve that problem it will avail us little to solve all others."

Seeing that forests, grazing lands and watersheds were in danger of impoverishment by exploiters, he and his able forester, Gifford Pinchot, began steering the nation conservation-wise by tightening Federal control over such lands. The President became interested in the conservation attitudes of John Muir by reading Muir's enthusiastic writings. He indicated to the famed naturalist through California Senator Chester Rowell that he desired to make a trip to Yosemite for the express purpose of "talking conservation" with him.

ROOSEVELT MAKES TRAVEL PLANS

Muir must have been thrilled at the prospects of a visit by the President, although he did not so express himself.

After receiving a personal letter from Roosevelt, he wrote to C.S. Sargent postponing their sailing date for Europe and the Orient, saying,

"An influential man from Washington wants to make a trip into the Sierra with me, and I might be able to do some forest good in freely talking around the campfire."

Some forest good was putting it mildly!

The President arrived dressed for the business at hand in his rough hunting clothes. He and Muir left the main party of dignitaries and slept on the ground at night, once in the snow, which delighted the President. The conversations around their Sierra campfires would probably fill several volumes, since both were prolific talkers.

Although we shall never know all that transpired on this memorial outing, there is much evidence of the good, which resulted from it.

John Muir was emphatic about the need for legislation to prevent archeological ruins from being destroyed by "pot hunters" and other collectors. The Petrified Forest and the Grand Canyon were foremost among specific areas mentioned.

Perhaps it was at this time that the two conceived a workable plan, which would vest the President with the necessary power to set apart as national monuments areas deemed nationally significant.

The purpose was, of course, to save time when areas were in immediate danger of invasion, and also to circumvent opposition in Congress, which might prevent many such areas from being established. The legislation was enacted in 1906 and is known today as the Antiquities Act.

The Birth of the Antiquities Act

Under various preemption acts, the public could obtain land cheaply or without actual cost. Intended to facilitate settlement of our new nation, these acts lent themselves beautifully to fraudulent practices.

Muir told the President of certain lumbering interests in California's redwood forests, which would engage sailors on incoming ships to file for the legal amount of redwood forestland and then immediately deed the land to the company which paid them $50.00 for their trouble.

This, and several other fraudulent practices which were brought to Roosevelt's attention accentuated his already determined opinion that action had to be taken as quickly as possible.

With the President's visit began a friendship with Muir that was carried on by mail though the years. T.R. had doubtlessly had a "bully good time" camping in Yosemite. He wrote Muir years later that he wished that once again they could camp underneath the sequoias.

"To Last Through the Ages"

En route to Washington the President stopped in Sacramento and in a speech, prevailed upon the citizens of this state to do all in their power to use their forests and streams wisely, to preserve the natural wealth.

He ended, "We are not building this country for a day. It is to last through the ages."

Back at the White House, the President attacked the many problems with renewed vigor. Not only his own staff was moved by his courageous attack on the misuse of our natural resources, but the public caught the enthusiastic approach to this real problem.

It was through such loyal support that he won battle after battle against an almost violent opposition of moneyed commercial interests.

During his administration, which ended in March 1909, Mesa Verde, Platt, Wind Cave and Crater Lake were established as national parks.

Having elected the areas to be established as national monuments while on his outing in Yosemite, he waited only for their boundary descriptions before signing the proclamations which withdrew them from public entry.

The establishment of the Grand Canyon as a park had long been the subject of debate. As far back as the Benjamin Harrison administration efforts had been made to establish it as a national park. Selfish interests succeeded in preventing it.

Chapter 2

THE TRIP BEGINS

On April 1, 1903, Theodore Roosevelt's train departed Washington, D.C. Six cars long, his train included a baggage car; a club car complete with barbershop; a diner car called the Gilsey; a large Pullman that carried reporters, photographers, telegraphers and Secret Service men; a sleeper car for White House staff; and Roosevelt's own personal "Elysian," an elegant Pullman car measuring seventy feet long and featuring two sleeping chambers, two bathrooms, a private kitchen, a dining room, a stateroom with picture windows and an airy rear platform from which he could deliver speeches in towns all across the West. He would not be joined by his wife or children, but he wrote to them frequently throughout the trip.

The first week of the journey was a whirlwind, featuring stops, speeches and events in Pennsylvania, Michigan, Illinois, North Dakota and Montana. On April 8, the train arrived in Wyoming. There, accompanied by well-known wildlife writer John Burroughs (the press having been left behind in Gardiner, Montana), Roosevelt would travel and camp in the backcountry with Burroughs until April 24.

As the Wyoming State Historical Society detailed:

> *While in the park, on April 16, Roosevelt wrote a detailed letter to Dr. C. Hart Merriam, a physician and early conservationist who had been head of the Section of Economic Ornithology in the Department of Agriculture and its successor agencies since 1885. Roosevelt reported on the numbers, habits and condition of game in Yellowstone, noting that*

A mounted deer and eagle can be seen displayed behind Roosevelt on the stage in Newcastle, Wyoming.

"coyotes wander about among…sleeping or feeding elk without attracting any attention whatever." He witnessed the attempt of a golden eagle to cut a yearling elk calf out of a herd and commented, "The elk far out-number all the other animals," estimating at least 15,000 within the park. He also mentioned that "around the hot springs the cougars are killing deer, antelope, and sheep…"

On April 24, Roosevelt dedicated a new arched gateway to the park with a short speech. Then he boarded his train, bound east for Omaha. Newcastle, Wyo. was one of many whistle stops the next day.

Sometimes Roosevelt made his speeches from the rear platform of the *Elysian*, his 70-foot long railroad car; at other times he made them from a decorated platform at the nearby depot. In Newcastle, as with many other stops, his path from train to platform was strewn with flowers. According to the April 26, 1903 edition of the Wyoming Tribune, *the platform itself was decorated with three statues: a deer, a bear and an eagle.*

Roosevelt on his horse near Fort Yellowstone, Wyoming. *Theodore Roosevelt Collection, Houghton Library, Harvard University.*

In 1907, Burroughs wrote a book called *Camping and Tramping with Roosevelt* that included many vivid recollections from the 1903 Roosevelt trip. In the absence of any first-person press reporting, it remains a vital piece of narrative. Following are several relevant passages from the book:

Part I

At the time I made the trip to Yellowstone Park with President Roosevelt in the spring of 1903, I promised some friends to write up my impressions of the President and of the Park, but I have been slow in getting around to it. The President himself, having the absolute leisure and peace of the White House, wrote his account of the trip nearly two years ago! But with the stress and strain of my life at "Slabsides,"—administering the affairs of so many of the wild creatures of the woods about me—I have not till this blessed season (fall of 1905) found the time to put on record an account of the most interesting thing I saw in that wonderful land, which, of course, was the President himself.

When I accepted his invitation I was well aware that during the journey I should be in a storm centre most of the time, which is not always a pleasant prospect to a man of my habits and disposition. The President himself is a good deal of a storm—a man of such abounding energy and ceaseless activity that he sets everything in motion around him wherever he goes. But I knew he would be pretty well occupied on his way to the Park in speaking to eager throngs and in receiving personal and political homage in the towns and cities we were to pass through. But when all this was over, and I found myself with him in the wilderness of the Park, with only the superintendent and a few attendants to help take up his tremendous personal impact, how was it likely to fare with a non-strenuous person like myself? I asked. I had visions of snow six and seven feet deep, where traveling could be done only upon snow-shoes, and I had never had the things on my feet in my life. If the infernal fires beneath, that keep the pot boiling so furiously in the Park, should melt the snows, I could see the party tearing along on horseback at a wolf-hunt pace over a rough country; and as I had not been on a horse's back since the President was born, how would it be likely to fare with me then?

I had known the President several years before he became famous, and we had had some correspondence on subjects of natural history. His interest in such themes is always very fresh and keen, and the main motive of his visit to the Park at this time was to see and study in its semi-domesticated

President Roosevelt is seen here laying the cornerstone of the gateway to Yellowstone National Park.

condition the great game which he had so often hunted during his ranch days; and he was kind enough to think it would be an additional pleasure to see it with a nature-lover like myself. For my own part, I knew nothing about big game, but I knew there was no man in the country with whom I should so like to see it as Roosevelt.

Some of our newspapers reported that the President intended to hunt in the Park. A woman in Vermont wrote me, to protest against the hunting, and hoped I would teach the President to love the animals as much as I did—as if he did not love them much more, because his love is founded upon knowledge, and because they had been a part of his life. She did not know that I was then cherishing the secret hope that I might be allowed to shoot a cougar or bobcat; but this fun did not come to me. The President said, "I will not fire a gun in the Park; then I shall have no explanations to make." Yet once I did hear him say in the wilderness, "I feel as if I ought to keep the camp in meat. I always have." I regretted that he could not do so on this occasion.

I have never been disturbed by the President's hunting trips. It is to such men as he that the big game legitimately belongs—men who regard it from the point of view of the naturalist as well as from that of the sportsman, who are interested in its preservation, and who share with the world the delight they experience in the chase. Such a hunter as Roosevelt is as far removed from the game-butcher as day is from night; and as for his killing of the "varmints"—bears, cougars, and bobcats—the fewer of these there are, the better for the useful and beautiful game.

The cougars, or mountain lions, in the Park certainly needed killing. The superintendent reported that he had seen where they had slain nineteen elk, and we saw where they had killed a deer and dragged its body across the trail. Of course, the President would not now on his hunting trips shoot an elk or a deer except to "keep the camp in meat," and for this purpose it is as legitimate as to slay a sheep or a steer for the table at home.

We left Washington on April 1, and strung several of the larger Western cities on our thread of travel—Chicago, Milwaukee, Madison, St. Paul, Minneapolis—as well as many lesser towns, in each of which the President made an address, sometimes brief, on a few occasions of an hour or more.

He gave himself very freely and heartily to the people wherever he went. He could easily match their Western cordiality and good-fellowship. Wherever his train stopped, crowds soon gathered, or had already gathered, to welcome him. His advent made a holiday in each town he visited. At all the principal stops the usual programme was: first, his reception by the committee of citizens appointed to receive him—they usually boarded his private car, and were one by one introduced to him; then a drive through the town with a concourse of carriages; then to the hall or open-air platform, where he spoke to the assembled throng; then to lunch or dinner; and then back to the train, and off for the next stop—a

Cowboys follow the train and cheer President Roosevelt near Hugo, Colorado.

round of hand-shaking, carriage-driving, speech-making each day. He usually spoke from eight to ten times every twenty-four hours, sometimes for only a few minutes from the rear platform of his private car, at others for an hour or more in some large hall. In Chicago, Milwaukee, and St. Paul, elaborate banquets were given him and his party, and on each occasion he delivered a carefully prepared speech upon questions that involved the policy of his administration. The throng that greeted him in the vast Auditorium in Chicago—that rose and waved and waved again—was one of the grandest human spectacles I ever witnessed.

PART II

We spent two nights in our Tower Falls camp, and on the morning of the third day set out on our return to Fort Yellowstone, pausing at Yancey's on our way, and exchanging greetings with the old frontiersman, who died a few weeks later.

While in camp we always had a big fire at night in the open near the tents, and around this we sat upon logs or camp-stools, and listened to the President's talk. What a stream of it he poured forth! and what a varied and picturesque stream!—anecdote, history, science, politics, adventure, literature; bits of his experience as a ranchman, hunter, Rough

Roosevelt on his horse in Laramie, Wyoming.

Rider, legislator, civil service commissioner, police commissioner, governor, president—the frankest confessions, the most telling criticisms, happy characterizations of prominent political leaders, or foreign rulers, or members of his own Cabinet; always surprising by his candor, astonishing by his memory, and diverting by his humor. His reading has been very wide, and he has that rare type of memory which retains details as well as mass and generalities. One night something started him off on ancient history, and one would have thought he was just fresh from his college course in history, the dates and names and events came so readily. Another time he discussed palæontology, and rapidly gave the outlines of the science, and the main facts, as if he had been reading up on the subject that very day. He sees things as wholes, and hence the relation of the parts comes easy to him.

At dinner, at the White House, the night before we started on the expedition, I heard him talking with a guest—an officer of the British army, who was just back from India. And the extent and variety of his information about India and Indian history and the relations of the British government to it were extraordinary. It put the British major on his mettle to keep pace with him.

One night in camp he told us the story of one of his Rough Riders who had just written him from some place in Arizona. The Rough Riders, wherever they are now, look to him in time of trouble. This one had come to grief in Arizona. He was in jail. So he wrote the President, and his letter ran something like this:—

Dear Colonel—I am in trouble. I shot a lady in the eye, but I did not intend to hit the lady; I was shooting at my wife.

And the presidential laughter rang out over the tree-tops. To another Rough Rider, who was in jail, accused of horse stealing, he had loaned two hundred dollars to pay counsel on his trial, and, to his surprise, in due time the money came back. The ex-Rough wrote that his trial never came off. "We elected our district attorney"; and the laughter again sounded, and drowned the noise of the brook near by.

On another occasion we asked the President if he was ever molested by any of the "bad men" of the frontier, with whom he had often come in contact. "Only once," he said. The cowboys had always treated him with the utmost courtesy, both on the round-up and in camp; "and the few real desperadoes I have seen were also perfectly polite." Once only was he maliciously shot at, and then not by a cowboy nor a bona fide "bad man,"

Theodore Roosevelt serving himself from a camp cook pot (location not identified).

but by a "broad-hatted ruffian of a cheap and common-place type." He had been compelled to pass the night at a little frontier hotel where the bar-room occupied the whole lower floor, and was, in consequence, the only place where the guests of the hotel, whether drunk or sober, could sit. As he entered the room, he saw that every man there was being terrorized by a half-drunken ruffian who stood in the middle of the floor with a revolver in each hand, compelling different ones to treat.

"I went and sat down behind the stove," said the President, "as far from him as I could get; and hoped to escape his notice. The fact that I wore glasses, together with my evident desire to avoid a fight, apparently gave him the impression that I could be imposed upon with impunity. He very soon approached me, flourishing his two guns, and ordered me to treat. I made no reply for some moments, when the fellow became so threatening that I saw something had to be done. The crowd, mostly sheep-herders and small grangers, sat or stood back against the wall, afraid to move. I was unarmed, and thought rapidly. Saying, 'Well, if I must, I must,' I got up as if to walk around him to the bar, then, as I got opposite him, I wheeled and fetched him as heavy a blow on the chin-point as I could strike. He went down like a steer before the axe, firing

"Pot luck" with the "boys"—President Roosevelt's cowboy breakfast at Hugo, Colorado.

both guns into the ceiling as he went. I jumped on him, and, with my knees on his chest, disarmed him in a hurry. The crowd was then ready enough to help me, and we hog-tied him and put him in an outhouse." The President alludes to this incident in his "Ranch Life," but does not give the details. It brings out his mettle very distinctly.

He told us in an amused way of the attempts of his political opponents at Albany, during his early career as a member of the Assembly, to besmirch his character. His outspoken criticisms and denunciations had become intolerable to them, so they laid a trap for him, but he was not caught. His innate rectitude and instinct for the right course saved him, as it has saved

Roosevelt standing on the porch of a Fort Yellowstone house. *Theodore Roosevelt Collection, Houghton Library, Harvard University.*

him many times since. I do not think that in any emergency he has to debate with himself long as to the right course to be pursued; he divines it by a kind of infallible instinct. His motives are so simple and direct that he finds a straight and easy course where another man, whose eye is less single, would flounder and hesitate.

One night he entertained us with reminiscences of the Cuban War, of his efforts to get his men to the firing line when the fighting began, of his greenness and general ignorance of the whole business of war, which in his telling was very amusing. He has probably put it all in his book about the war, a work I have not yet read. He described the look of the slope of Kettle Hill when they were about to charge up it, how the grass was combed and rippled by the storm of rifle bullets that swept down it. He said, "I was conscious of being pale when I looked at it and knew that in a few moments we were going to charge there." The men of his regiment were all lying flat upon the ground, and it became his duty to walk along their front and encourage them and order them up on their feet. "Get up, men, get up!" One big fellow did not rise. Roosevelt stooped down and took hold of him and ordered him up. Just at that moment a bullet struck the man and went the entire length of him. He never rose.

Roosevelt's train near the Colorado Rockies.

On this or on another occasion when a charge was ordered, he found himself a hundred yards or more in advance of his regiment, with only the color bearer and one corporal with him. He said they planted the flag there, while he rushed back to fetch the men. He was evidently pretty hot. "Can it be that you flinched when I led the way!" and then they came with a rush. On the summit of Kettle Hill he was again in advance of his men, and as he came up, three Spaniards rose out of the trenches and deliberately fired at him at a distance of only a few paces, and then turned and fled. But a bullet from his revolver stopped one of them. He seems to have been as much exposed to bullets in this engagement as Washington was at Braddock's defeat, and to have escaped in the same marvelous manner.

The President unites in himself powers and qualities that rarely go together. Thus, he has both physical and moral courage in a degree rare in history. He can stand calm and unflinching in the path of a charging grizzly, and he can confront with equal coolness and determination the predaceous corporations and money powers of the country.

He unites the qualities of the man of action with those of the scholar and writer—another very rare combination. He unites the instincts and accomplishments of the best breeding and culture with the broadest democratic sympathies and affiliations. He is as happy with a frontiersman like Seth Bullock as with a fellow Harvard man, and Seth Bullock is happy, too.

He unites great austerity with great good nature. He unites great sensibility with great force and will power. He loves solitude, and he loves to be in the thick of the fight. His love of nature is equaled only by his love of the ways and arts of men.

He is doubtless the most vital man on the continent, if not on the planet, to-day. He is many-sided, and every side throbs with his tremendous life and energy; the pressure is equal all around. His interests are as keen in natural history as in economics, in literature as in statecraft, in the young poet as in the old soldier, in preserving peace as in preparing for war. And he can turn all his great power into the new channel on the instant. His interest in the whole of life, and in the whole life of the nation, never flags for a moment. His activity is tireless. All the relaxation he needs or craves is a change of work. He is like the farmer's fields, that only need a rotation of crops. I once heard him say that all he cared about being President was just "the big work."

During this tour through the West, lasting over two months, he made nearly three hundred speeches; and yet on his return Mrs. Roosevelt told me he looked as fresh and unworn as when he left home.

President Roosevelt and Yellowstone's superintendent, Major John Pitcher, on horseback at Liberty Cap in Wyoming. *Theodore Roosevelt Collection, Houghton Library, Harvard University.*

The second morning at Norris's one of our teamsters, George Marvin, suddenly dropped dead from some heart affection, just as he had finished caring for his team. It was a great shock to us all. I never saw a better man with a team than he was. I had ridden on the seat beside him all the day previous. On one of the "formations" our teams had got mired in the soft, putty-like mud, and at one time it looked as if they could never extricate themselves, and I doubt if they could have, had it not been for the skill with which Marvin managed them. We started for the Grand Cañon up the Yellowstone that morning, and, in order to give myself a walk over the crisp snow in the clear, frosty air, I set out a little while in advance of the teams. As I did so, I saw the President, accompanied by one of the teamsters, walking hurriedly toward the barn to pay his last respects to the body of Marvin. After we had returned to Mammoth Hot Springs, he made inquiries for the young woman to whom he had been told that Marvin was engaged to be married. He looked her up, and sat a long time with her in her home, offering his sympathy, and speaking words of consolation. The act shows the depth and breadth of his humanity.

At the Cañon Hotel the snow was very deep, and had become so soft from the warmth of the earth beneath, as well as from the sun above, that we could only reach the brink of the Cañon on skis. The President and Major Pitcher had used skis before, but I had not, and, starting out without the customary pole, I soon came to grief. The snow gave way beneath me, and I was soon in an awkward predicament. The more I struggled, the lower my head and shoulders went, till only my heels, strapped to those long timbers, protruded above the snow. To reverse my position was impossible till some one came and reached me the end of a pole, and pulled me upright. But I very soon got the hang of the things, and the President and I quickly left the superintendent behind. I think I could have passed the President, but my manners forbade. He was heavier than I was, and broke in more. When one of his feet would go down half a yard or more, I noted with admiration the skilled diplomacy he displayed in extricating it. The tendency of my

Roosevelt's train near Fairmont, Nebraska. *Theodore Roosevelt Collection, Houghton Library, Harvard University.*

skis was all the time to diverge, and each to go off at an acute angle to my main course, and I had constantly to be on the alert to check this tendency.

Paths had been shoveled for us along the brink of the Cañon, so that we got the usual views from the different points. The Cañon was nearly free from snow, and was a grand spectacle, by far the grandest to be seen in the Park. The President told us that once, when pressed for meat, while returning through here from one of his hunting trips, he had made his way down to the river that we saw rushing along beneath us, and had caught some trout for dinner. Necessity alone could induce him to fish.

Across the head of the Falls there was a bridge of snow and ice, upon which we were told that the coyotes passed. As the season progressed, there would come a day when the bridge would not be safe. It would be interesting to know if the coyotes knew when this time arrived.

Near the falls of the Yellowstone, as at other places we had visited, a squad of soldiers had their winter quarters. The President called on them, as he had called upon the others, looked over the books they had to read, examined their housekeeping arrangements, and conversed freely with them.

In front of the hotel were some low hills separated by gentle valleys. At the President's suggestion, he and I raced on our skis down those inclines. We had only to stand up straight, and let gravity do the rest. As we were going swiftly down the side of one of the hills, I saw out of the corner of my eye the President taking a header into the snow. The snow had given way beneath him, and nothing could save him from taking the plunge. I don't know whether I called out, or only thought, something about the downfall of the administration. At any rate, the administration was down, and pretty well buried, but it was quickly on its feet again, shaking off the snow with a boy's laughter. I kept straight on, and very soon the laugh was on me, for the treacherous snow sank beneath me, and I took a header, too.

"Who is laughing now, Oom John?" called out the President.

The spirit of the boy was in the air that day about the Cañon of the Yellowstone, and the biggest boy of us all was President Roosevelt.

The snow was getting so soft in the middle of the day that our return to the Mammoth Hot Springs could no longer be delayed. Accordingly, we were up in the morning, and ready to start on the home journey, a distance of twenty miles, by four o'clock. The snow bore up the horses well till mid-forenoon, when it began to give way beneath them. But by very careful management we pulled through without serious delay, and were back again at the house of Major Pitcher in time for luncheon, being the only outsiders who had ever made the tour of the Park so early in the season.

This magazine cover shows a family of bears dressed as humans near railroad tracks, with the youngest cub crying. A train labeled "Presidential Special" has just passed, and standing on the back of the last car is President Theodore Roosevelt, holding papers labeled "Speeches." The mother bear indicates that Roosevelt is on a campaign tour rather than a hunting expedition. Some in the press had a field day with this trip, as this cover of the then popular political satire magazine *Puck* illustrates.

A few days later I bade good-by to the President, who went on his way to California, while I made a loop of travel to Spokane, and around through Idaho and Montana, and had glimpses of the great, optimistic, sunshiny West that I shall not soon forget.

Yellowstone Park, Wyoming, April 16, 1903.

DARLING ETHEL:
I wish you could be here and see how tame all the wild creatures are. As I write a dozen of deer have come down to the parade grounds, right in front of the house, to get the hay; they are all looking at the bugler, who has begun to play the "retreat."

Chapter 3
A BADGER AND A GRAND CANYON

From Yellowstone, Roosevelt's train headed west, making stops in Wyoming, Nebraska, Iowa and Missouri, at which point the trip hit its halfway point. But May 3, the train had picked up a special passenger who would eventually make it back to the White House. It happened in the small town of Sharon Springs, Kansas, as Roosevelt himself recounted, describing the Sunday church service he attended:

> There were two very nice little girls standing in the aisle beside me. I invited them in and we all three sang out of the same hymn book. They were in their Sunday best and their brown sunburned little arms and faces had been scrubbed till they almost shone. When church was over, I shook hands with the three preachers and all the congregation, whose buggies, ranch wagons, and dispirited-looking saddle ponies were tied to everything available in the village. I got a ride myself in the afternoon, and on returning, found that all the population that had not left had gathered solemnly around the train. Among the [crowd gathered on the train platform] was a little girl who asked me if I would like a baby badger which she said her brother Josiah had just caught. I said I would, and an hour or two later, the badger turned up from the little girl's father's ranch…The little girl had several other little girls with her, all in clean starched Sunday clothes and ribbon-tied pigtails. One of them was the sheriff's daughter, and I saw her nudging the sheriff, trying to make some request, which he refused. So I asked what it was and I found that the seven little girls were exceedingly anxious to see the

inside of my [train] *car, and accordingly I took them all in. The interior arrangements struck them as being literally palatial.*

Roosevelt gave the girls flowers and a silver and gold medal he had been presented in Chicago on the trip. And thenceforth Josiah the badger was along for the rest of the ride, a new pet for the president's children back in D.C. Roosevelt himself would feed the animal cut-up potatoes and milk throughout the journey, and members of the press helped tend to him.

From left to right: Governor Brodie of Arizona (left), T.R. and Secretary William Loeb, with backs to the camera, at Grand Canyon, Arizona.

From Kansas, the train made stops in Denver, Santa Fe and Albuquerque and then arrived at the Grand Canyon on May 6, like Yellowstone another first-time visit for Roosevelt.

According to a local newspaper, the *Coconino Sun*, he spent just eight and a half hours at the Canyon, after arriving just after 9:30 a.m. on May 6 (after a brief stop in Flagstaff). He went on a horseback trip, gave his speech, received some local honors and gifts, handed out high school diplomas, went on a rim excursion to Grandview Point, held a reception for his fellow Rough Riders at 5:30 p.m. and left promptly at 6:00 p.m.

Following is a complete transcript of his May 6, 1903 Grand Canyon speech, taken down by a reporter from the *Coconino Sun*:

> *Mr. Governor, and you my Fellow Citizens, My Fellow Americans, Men and Women of Arizona: I am glad to be in Arizona today. It was from Arizona that so many gallant men came into the regiment, which I had the honor to command. Arizona sent men who won glory on hard-fought fields, and men to whom came a glorious and an honorable death fighting for the flag of their country, and as long as I live it will be to me an inspiration to have served with Bucky [sic] O'Neill. (Applause.) I have met so many comrades whom I prize for whom I feel only respect and admiration, and I shall not particularize among them except to say that there is no one for whom I feel more of respect than for your governor. (Applause.) I remember when I first joined the regiment that all of us were new to one another, but as soon as I saw the colonel (he was then major) I made up my mind I could tie to him. (Cries of "Good!" Applause.)*
>
> *It is a pleasure to be in Arizona. I have never been in it before. Arizona is one of the regions from which I expect most development through the wise action of the national congress in passing the irrigation act. (Applause.) The first and biggest experiment now in view under that act is the one that we are trying in Arizona. I look forward to the effects of irrigation partly as applied through the government, still more as applied by individuals, and especially by associations of individuals, profiting by the example of the government and possibly by help from it—I look forward to the effects of irrigation as being of greater consequence to all this region of country in the next fifty years than any other movement whatsoever. I think that irrigation counts for more toward the achieving of the permanent good results for the community.*
>
> *I shall not try to greet in particular the members of my regiment now. I shall see them at half past five in my car. I have come here to see the Grand Canyon of Arizona, because in that canyon Arizona has a natural wonder, which, so far as I know, is in kind absolutely unparalleled throughout the rest*

Throughout the nearly nine-week trip, Roosevelt, childlike, would frequently visit the front of the train to ride with the crew.

of the world. (Applause.) I shall not attempt to describe it, because I cannot. I could not choose words that would convey or that could convey to any outsider what that canyon is. I want to ask you to do one thing in connection with it in your own interest and in the interest of the country—to keep this great wonder of nature as it now is. (Applause.) I was delighted to learn of the wisdom of the Santa Fe railroad people in deciding not to build their hotel on the brink of the canyon. I hope you will not have a building of any kind, not a summer cottage, a hotel or anything else to mar the wonderful grandeur, the sublimity, the loneliness and beauty of the canyon. Leave it as it is. Man cannot improve on it; not a bit. The ages have been at work on it and man can only mar it. What you can do is to keep it for your children and your children's children and for all who come after you, as one of the great sights which every American, if he can travel at all, should see.

Keep the Grand Canyon of Arizona as it is. We have gotten past the stage, my fellow citizens, when we are to be pardoned if we simply treat any part of our country as something to be skinned for two or three years for the use of the present generation. Whether it is the forest, the water, the scenery, whatever it is, handle it so that your children's children will get the benefit of it. Handle it that way. If irrigation, apply it under circumstances that will make it of benefit, not to the speculators to get profit out of it for two or three years, but handle it so that it will be of use to the homemaker; to the man who comes to live here and to have his children stay after him; handle it so as to be of use to him and those who come after him. Keep the forests in the same way. Preserve them for that use, but use them so that they will not be squandered; will not be wasted; so that they will be of benefit to the Arizona of 1952 [sic] as well as the Arizona of 1903.

I want to say a word of welcome to the Indians here. In my regiment I had a good many Indians. They were good enough to fight and to die, and they are good enough to have me treat them exactly as square as any white man. There are a good many problems in connection with the Indians. You have got to save them from corruption, save them from brutality, and I regret to say that at times we have to save them from the unregulated Eastern philanthropist, because in everything we have to remember that although perhaps the worst quality in which to approach any question is hardness of heart, I do not know that it does so much damage as selfishness of head. All I ask is a square deal for every man. Give him a fair chance; do not let him wrong anyone, and do not let him be wronged. Help as far as you can, without hurting in helping him, for the only way to help a man in the end is to help a man to help himself. Never forget that you have to have two sets of qualities; the qualities that we include under the names of decency, honesty, morality, that make a man a decent husband, a good father, a good neighbor, fair and square in his dealings with all men, and in his dealings with the state: and then, furthermore, the qualities that have to be shown by every man who is to do this work in the world. Virtue is good, but the virtue that sits at home in its own parlor and talks about how bad the world is, never did anything and never will. I want to see the qualities that the men of '61 to '65 had, my comrades. You had to have a man patriotic in those days, but it did not make any difference how patriotic he was, if he did not fight he was no good. So it is with citizenship. I want to see decency and then I want

President Roosevelt speaking to the great crowds in front of the capitol in Denver, Colorado.

to see the hardy virtues; the virtues we speak of when we describe anyone as a good man. I am glad to see you today. I wish you well with all my heart. I know that your future will justify all the hopes we have.

And then it was on to California.

Chapter 4
ARRIVING IN CALIFORNIA

On May 7, just one week before meeting Muir, Roosevelt's train traveled through the Mojave Desert and brought the president into California for the first time. It would be a busy several days, starting with a short speech in the dusty little town of Barstow, where thousands of thrilled citizens greeted him. Speaking from the platform on the back of his train car, he told the people:

> *This is the first time I have ever been to California, and I cannot say to you how much I have looked forward to making the trip. I can tell you now with absolute certainty that I will have enjoyed it to the full when I get through.*
>
> *I have felt that the events of the last five or six years have been steadily hastening the day when the Pacific will loom in the world's commerce as the Atlantic now looms, and I have wished greatly to see these marvelous communities growing up on the Pacific Slope. There are plenty of things that to you seem matters of course, that I have read about and know about from reading, and yet when I see them they strike me as very wonderful—the way the railroads have been thrust across the deserts, until now we come to the border of that wonderful flower land, the wonderful land of your state.*
>
> *One thing that strikes me more than anything else as I go through the country—as I said I have never been on the Pacific Slope; the Rocky Mountain States and the States of the great plains I know quite as well as I know the Eastern seaboard; I have worked with the men, played with*

Roosevelt's train approaching Redlands, California. *Theodore Roosevelt Collection, Houghton Library, Harvard University.*

them, fought with them; I know them all through—the thing that strikes me most as I go through this country and meet the men and women of the country, is the essential unity of all Americans. Down at bottom we are the same people all through. (Applause) That is not merely a unity of section; it is a unity of class. For my good fortune I have been thrown into intimate

President Roosevelt welcomed by California—cheered by thousands at Redlands.

relationship, into intimate personal friendship, with many men of many different occupations, and my faith is firm that we shall come unscathed out of all our difficulties here in America, because I think that the average American is a decent fellow, and that the prime thing in getting him to get on well with the other average American is to have each remember that the other is a decent fellow, and try to look at the problems a little from the other's standpoint. (Applause)

I am speaking here to the men who have done their part in the tremendous development of this country—railroad men, the ranchers, the people who have built up this country. Something can be done by law to help in such development, something can be done by the administration of the law; but in the last analysis we have to rely upon the average citizenship of the country to work out the salvation of the nation. (Applause) Back of the law stands the man; just exactly as in battle it is the man behind the gun that counts most, even more than the gun. (Applause) So it is the man and woman, it is the average type of manhood and womanhood, that makes the

Roosevelt on May 7, 1903, speaking at Redlands just after first arriving in California.

State great in the end. In the individual nothing can take the place of his own qualities; in the community nothing can take the place of the qualities of the average citizen. The law can do something, but the law never yet made a fool wise or a coward brave or a weakling strong. The law can endeavor to secure a fair show for every man so far as it is in the wit of man to secure such a fair show, but it must then remain for the man himself to show the stuff there is in him; and if the stuff is not in him, you cannot get it out of him. (Applause)

I believe in the future of this country because I believe in the men and women whom we are developing in the country. I am more glad than I can say for being in California. I thank you for coming out here to greet me. I wish you well with all my heart for the future. (Cheers and applause)

Shortly after that, the train made a short stop in Victorville, and then it was on to Redlands, where a major celebration had been planned.

In 1903, Redlands was known as the "Land of Flowers" and the "Naval Orange Capital of the World." Thanks to William McKinley's protective tariffs that kept the foreign oranges out of America, Redlands had become a wealthy place, and so the former president was revered there. When McKinley had visited in 1901, he was treated like a king, with the streets covered in rose petals so thick that the president's carriage wheels could not even be heard against the ground.

Four months later, McKinley was dead, shot by a crazed anarchist, and now Roosevelt was president. Exactly two years after, here was Teddy, who unveiled a memorial bust of McKinley atop a granite pedestal engraved "Patriot, Statesman, Martyr" before giving a powerful speech at the old Casa Loma Hotel:

Mr. Chairman, Mr. Mayor, Mr. Governor, and You, My Fellow-Americans, Men and Women of California: I am glad indeed to have the chance to visit this wonderful and beautiful State. And yet, first, let me tell you, my fellow-citizens, I did not need to come here to be one of you and devoted to your interests. I know California. I know what her sons and daughters are and what they have done, for if I did not I would augur myself but a poor American. Rarely have I enjoyed a day more than this. I waked up coming through the Mojave Desert, and all that desert needs is water, and I believe you are going to get it. Then we came down into this wonderful garden spot, and though I had been told all about it, told about the fruits and the flowers, told of the wonderful fertility and thought

I knew about it, it was not possible in advance to realize all the fertility, all the beauty, that I was to see. Indeed I congratulate myself on having had the chance to visit you. (Applause) Coming today over the mountain range, coming down here, seeing what you have done, makes me realize more and more how much this whole country should lay stress on what can be done by the wise use of water, and, therefore, the wise use of the forests on the mountains. (Applause) When I come to California I can sit at the feet of Gamaliel and learn about forestry and water. I do not have to preach it.

All I can do is to ask you to go ahead and follow your own best practice. The people of our country have grown to realize and are more and more in practice showing that they realize how indispensable it is to preserve the great forests on the mountains and to use aright the water supply that those forests conserve. This whole country here in Southern California shows what can be done by irrigation, what can be done by settlers foresighted enough to use the resources in such way as to perpetuate and better, not exhaust, them. We have passed the time when we could afford to let any man skin the country and leave it. (Applause) Forestry, irrigation, all the efforts of the nation and the State governments, all the efforts of individuals and of local associations are to be bent to the object of building up the interests of the home-maker. The man we want to favor is the man who comes to live, and whose interest it is that his children and his children's children shall enjoy to an even greater degree what he has enjoyed himself. He is the man whom we must encourage in every possible way; and it is because he is awake to his true interests that the marvelous progress has been made, largely through forestry, largely through irrigation, here in California and elsewhere in the mighty Western land, which forms the major half of this republic. (Applause) I think our citizens are more and more realizing that they wish to perpetuate the things that are of use and also the things that are of beauty. You in California are preserving your great natural scenery, your great objects of nature, your valleys, your giant trees. You are preserving them because you realize that beauty has its place as well as use, because you wish to make of this State even more than it now is the garden spot of the continent, the garden spot of the world.

This same day, it was on to nearby San Bernardino, the Riverside. En route, approaching the city, the train made a special stop near the corner of Victoria Avenue and Myrtle Avenue in Riverside, where Roosevelt planted a Mexican fan palm tree, which still stands today. Nearing dark, the train arrived in Riverside at the beautiful Mission Inn. That evening, more than four hundred attended a banquet held in his honor. The president stayed in a four-room suite on the main floor of the hotel, later named the "Presidential Suite."

Roosevelt, with back to the camera, talking to an engineer near Redlands, California. *Theodore Roosevelt Collection, Houghton Library, Harvard University.*

This was Roosevelt's May 7 address in Riverside:

Mr. Mayor, and You, My Fellow-Citizens: I have enjoyed to the full getting into your beautiful State. I had read about what I should expect here in Southern California, but I had formed no idea of the fertility of your soil, the beauty of your scenery, or the wonderful manner in which the full advantage of that soil had been taken by man. Here I am in the pioneer community of irrigated fruit growing in California. In many other parts of the country I have had to preach irrigation. Here you practice it (applause), and all I have to say here is that I earnestly wish that I could have many another community learn from you how you have handled your business. Not only has it been most useful, but it is astonishing to see how with the use you have combined beauty. You have made of this city and its surroundings a veritable little paradise.

It has been delightful to see you. Today has been my first day in California. I need hardly say that I have enjoyed it to the full. I am glad to

President Roosevelt replanting the original navel orange tree in front of old Adobe and Campanile, at Glenwood Inn, Riverside, California, where he spent the night of May 7, 1903.

be welcomed by all of you, but most of all by the men of the Grand Army, and after them by my own comrades of the National Guard, and I have been particularly pleased to pass between the rows of school children. I like your stock and I am glad it is not dying out. (Applause)

I shall not try this evening to do more than say to you a word of thanks for your greeting to me. I admire your country, but I admire most of all the men and women of the country. It is a good thing to grow citrus fruits, but it is even a better thing to have the right kind of citizenship. I think you have been able to combine the very extraordinary material prosperity with that form of the higher life, which must be built upon material prosperity if it is to amount to what it should in the long run.

I am glad to have seen you. I thank you for coming here to greet me. I wish you well at all times and in every way, and I bid you good luck and good night.

The next morning, May 8, prior to leaving Riverside, Roosevelt participated in a tree planting ceremony. He transplanted one of Riverside's two famous parent navel orange trees in the Court of the Birds. These trees had launched a citrus economy that made Riverside the richest American city of the 1890s (and one of them still remains on display in the city, visible through lock and key). And then it was yet another busy day, with speeches and events in Pasadena and, finally, Los Angeles.

A stop was also made at Claremont, where the president spoke to the students of Pomona College, the president of which, John D. Gates, was an old friend of his:

There is not much need of educating the body if one pursues certain occupations, but the minute that you come to people who pursue a sedentary life, there is great need for educating the body. All must recognize that if we think of it. The man that is the ideal citizen, is the man who, in the event of trial, in the event of a call from this country, can respond to that call. When the call comes, you need not only fiery enthusiasm, but you need the body containing that fiery enthusiasm to be sufficiently hardy to bear it up. Every college should aid, from its intellectual side, from the intellectual standpoint, to add to the sum of productive scholarship of the nation. You should turn your attention to the things that you find naturally at hand, or to which your mind naturally turns, and try, in dealing with that, to deal so in a fresh way that the net income shall be an addition to the world's stock of wisdom and knowledge. Every college should strive to develop among its students the capacity to do good original work.

The navel parent orange tree planted by Roosevelt.

The train ran through the picturesque San Gabriel Valley to Pasadena, where it visited for two hours. The businesses and residences along the route over which the president was driven displayed American flags and bunting. As the president passed the Elks Lodge building, Congressman MacLachlan

The famous Feast of Flowers in Los Angeles, reviewed by President Roosevelt.

presented him with a gold key, a facsimile of the one that opened the Elks Lodge room. At the Wilson High School, the president passed under a floral archway that extended for two blocks. The front of the archway was a solid mass of flowers from base to top, and festoons of very colorful roses were draped across from curb to curb. Baskets of flowers on Similac's twined poles extended from the high school building, and solid banks of roses covered the walls of the façade from base to cupola. Directly in front of the stand from which the president made a brief address, there were 2,500 schoolchildren, each one carrying a long light pole with the national colors waving from the top and palms and wreaths of flowers from the center. After the address, the president was driven through the city, a brief stop being made at the home of Mrs. Garfield, the widow of the late president. From the top of Raymond Hill, the president had a splendid view of the fertile San Gabriel Valley.

When the train pulled in at La Grande Station in Los Angeles, thousands of people blocked the streets on every side. Former members of the Rough Riders regiment (a detachment of Troops D, C and G) and Teddy's Terrors, a political club of Los Angeles businessmen, wearing the Rough Rider uniform, formed on either side of the platform and kept the crowd back.

Roosevelt speaking in Claremont, California.

The president was driven directly to the Westminster Hotel, where lunch was served. The people along the route continuously cheered him. The annual Fiesta de Las Flores, the chief feature of which was the elaborate floral parade, was arranged this year to coincide with the visit of the president.

Unusual efforts had been made by the fiesta committee to make this feature of the celebration particularly attractive, a sort of expression of the floral wealth of California. The parade occurred in the afternoon and was reviewed by the president. Returning to the hotel, he dined with a large delegation of state officials and invited guests. In the evening, he reviewed the electrical parade, which was the closing feature of the day. This is the speech Roosevelt gave to the people of Los Angeles:

> *I greet you and thank you for the enjoyment you have given me today. I cannot say how I have appreciated being here in your beautiful State and your beautiful city. I do not remember ever seeing quite the parallel to the procession I have just witnessed. (Applause) I find, men and women of California, that California believes implicitly in two of my own favorite beliefs—the navy and irrigation. (Applause) The navy, because this country is one of the great leading nations of mankind and is bound to become ever greater as the years roll by, and therefore it must have a navy corresponding to its position. (Applause) Moreover, we as a nation front two great oceans, and we must have a navy capable of asserting our position alike on the Pacific and the Atlantic. (Applause) This year we have begun the preparations for the completion of the Isthmian Canal. (Applause) That is important commercially; it will become even more important should we ever become involved in war, because holding that canal it would be open to our own warships and closed to those of any hostile power. (Applause) I want a navy, I want to see the American republic with a fighting navy, because I never wish to see us take a position that we cannot maintain. I do not believe in a bluff. I feel about a nation as we all feel about a man; let him not say anything that he cannot make good, and having said it let him make it good. (Applause) I believe in doing all we can to avoid a quarrel, to avoid trouble; I believe in speaking courteously of all the other peoples of mankind, of scrupulously refraining from wronging them and of seeing that in return they do not wrong us. (Applause) I believe in the Monroe doctrine, and I believe in it not as an empty formula of words, but as something we are ready to make good by deeds, and therefore I believe in having an adequate navy with which to make that doctrine good. More than that, here on the Pacific, the greatest of the oceans, we as a nation are growing by leaps and*

Roosevelt visiting the mission at Santa Barbara, California.

by bounds, our interests increasing with ever accelerating rapidity, and if we are to protect those interests, and to take the position we should take, we must see that the growth of the navy takes place with equal rapidity with the growth of the interests that it is to protect.

When I come to speak of the preservation of the forests, of the preservation of the waters, of the use of the waters from the mountains and of the waters

Roosevelt giving a speech in Santa Barbara.

obtained by artesian wells, I only have to appeal to your own knowledge, to your experience. I have been passing through a veritable garden of the earth yesterday and today, here in the southern half of California, and it has been made such by the honesty and wisdom of your people, and by the way in which you have preserved your waters and utilized them. I ask that you simply, keep on as you have begun, and that you let the rest of the nation follow suit. We must preserve the forests to preserve the waters, which are themselves preserved by the forests, if we wish to make this country as a whole blossom as you have made this part of California blossom.

In saying good-by to you I want to say that it has been the greatest pleasure to see you, and I am glad, my fellow-Americans, to think that you and I are citizens of the same country.

The train left Los Angeles at 5:00 a.m. on May 9 and next stopped up along the coast in the city of Ventura. The entrance to the city was through a magnificent floral arch, the gates of which were swung wide by members of the board of town trustees and the board of supervisors. The route along the main streets was packed with several thousand people, who accorded the president an enthusiastic ovation. A stop was made before the column of pioneers, of which body the president was elected as an honorary member, being decorated with the badge of the association. At the old mission, the president climbed to the belfry and listened to the wooden bells that have been chimed for more than a century. He also visited the Bard Memorial Hospital and made a speech on a platform in front of the plaza school. Here he got his first glimpse ever of the Pacific Ocean, which he mentioned in his speech:

I have enjoyed to the full the time I have spent in your wonderful and beautiful State. Just now I have for the first time in my life seen the greatest of all the oceans. (Applause) When I come here to California I am not in the West, I am west of the West. It is just California. And yet, oh, my fellow-countrymen, the thing after all that strikes me most is the fact that when I speak to you who dwell beside the Pacific, I, who have come from beside the Atlantic, am speaking to my own people, with the same thoughts and the same ideals. (Applause) How could it be otherwise in a community where I am greeted first by the men of the Grand Army, by the men who, in the days that tried men's souls, so worked and so fought that today we have one country and one flag; and each of us here, each man and each woman, is walking with head erect because of citizenship in the proudest and greatest republic upon which the sun has ever shone.

Santa Barbara was reached at eleven o'clock in the morning. Carriages awaited the president at Montecito, and he was escorted to the city by a large delegation of citizens, mounted police and forest rangers. On the way,

President Roosevelt speaks at Surf, California, just outside Santa Barbara on May 9, 1903. *Theodore Roosevelt Collection, Houghton Library, Harvard University.*

he was taken over drives in one of the most beautiful suburbs and over a portion of the Mountain Boulevard, which commands a view of the city, sea and Channel Islands. He addressed about fifteen thousand people on the Plaza Delmar and witnessed a parade. The president then visited points of historical interest. He spent considerable time at the old mission as the guest of the Franciscan fathers and saw the sacred burying grounds where hundreds of old padres have been buried during the past century and which no woman has ever been permitted to enter. A stop was made at San Luis Obispo, where a great crowd welcomed the president.

On May 9, 1903, in the morning *Tribune* newspaper, there was this announcement regarding the president's San Luis Obispo appearance: "It is a special request of private secretary Loeb that no fireworks or firearms of any character whatsoever be exploded during the president's visit. Anyone who violates or attempts to violate this regulation will be promptly arrested." Clearly, this was in reaction to the fact that Roosevelt's predecessor, William

Roosevelt and party at the Old Mission of the Franciscan Fathers, Santa Barbara. *Theodore Roosevelt Collection, Houghton Library, Harvard University.*

A bouquet given to President Roosevelt from a child in the California desert.

McKinley, who had also visited San Luis Obispo by rail, had been assassinated by a gun-wielding anarchist in New York. Despite the tumultuous receptions Roosevelt was regularly receiving, his team was on constant guard given the circumstances that had resulted in Roosevelt becoming president two years earlier. Throughout the trip, several potential assassination plots were thought to have been thwarted.

In Monterey, the trip came to a rest for a few days at the Hotel Del Monte resort (the struture of which still stands today as the administrative offices and hotel for the Naval Postgraduate School of the United States Navy). From here, Roosevelt, always a prolific man of letters, wrote to his children to give them updates on his trip:

Del Monte, Cal., May 10, 1903.
Darling Ethel:

I have thought it very good of you to write me so much. Of course I am feeling rather fagged, and the next four days, which will include San Francisco, will be tiresome; but I am very well. This is a beautiful hotel in which we are spending Sunday, with gardens and a long seventeen-mile drive beside the beach and the rocks and among the pines and cypresses. I went on horseback. My horse was a little beauty, spirited, swift, sure-footed and enduring. As is usually the case here they had a great deal of silver on the bridle and headstall, and much carving on the saddle. We had some splendid gallops. By the way, tell mother that everywhere out here, from the Mississippi to the Pacific, I have seen most of the girls riding astride, and most of the grown-up women. I must say I think it very much better for the horses' backs. I think by the time that you are an old lady the side-saddle will almost have vanished—I am sure I hope so. I have forgotten whether you like the sidesaddle or not.

It was very interesting going through New Mexico and seeing the strange old civilization of the desert, and next day the Grand Canyon of Arizona, wonderful and beautiful beyond description. I could have sat and looked at it for days. It is a tremendous chasm, a mile deep and several miles wide, the cliffs carved into battlements, amphitheatres, towers and pinnacles, and the coloring wonderful, red and yellow and gray and green. Then we went through the desert, passed across the Sierras and came into this semi-tropical country of southern California, with palms and orange groves and olive orchards and immense quantities of flowers.

Del Monte, Cal., May 10, 1903.
Blessed Kermit:

The last weeks' travel I have really enjoyed. Last Sunday and today (Sunday) and also on Wednesday at the Grand Canyon I had long rides, and the country has been strange and beautiful. I have collected a variety of treasures, which I shall have to try to divide up equally among you children. One treasure, by the way, is a very small badger, which I named Josiah, and he is now called Josh for short. He is very cunning and I hold him in my arms and pet him. I hope he will grow up friendly—that is if the poor little fellow lives to grow up at all. Dulany is taking excellent care of him, and we feed him on milk and potatoes. I have enjoyed meeting an old classmate of mine at Harvard. He was heavyweight boxing champion when I was in college.

I was much interested in your seeing the wild deer. That was quite remarkable. Today, by the way, as I rode along the beach I saw seals, cormorants, gulls and ducks, all astonishingly tame.

Del Monte, Cal., May 10, 1903.
Blessed Archie:

I think it was very cunning for you and Quentin to write me that letter together. I wish you could have been with me today on Algonquin, for we had a perfectly lovely ride. Dr. Rixey and I were on two very handsome horses, with Mexican saddles and bridles; the reins of very slender leather with silver rings. The road led through pine and cypress forests and along the beach. The surf was beating on the rocks in one place and right between two of the rocks where I really did not see how anything could swim a seal appeared and stood up on his tail half out of the foaming water and flapped his flippers, and was as much at home as anything could be. Beautiful gulls flew close to us all around, and cormorants swam along the breakers or walked along the beach.

I have a number of treasures to divide among you children when I get back. One of the treasures is Bill the Lizard. He is a little live lizard, called a horned frog, very cunning, who lives in a small box. The little badger, Josh, is very well and eats milk and potatoes. We took him out and gave him a run in the sand today. So far he seems as friendly as possible. When he feels hungry he squeals and the colored porters insist that he says "Du-la-ny, Du-la-ny," because Dulany is very good to him and takes care of him.

Del Monte, Cal., May 10, 1903.
Dearest Qunety-Quee (author's note: he is referring to Quentin):

I loved your letter. I am very homesick for mother and for you children; but I have enjoyed this week's travel. I have been among the orange groves, where the trees have oranges growing thick upon them, and there are more flowers than you have ever seen. I have a gold top which I shall give you if mother thinks you can take care of it. Perhaps I shall give you a silver bell instead. Whenever I see a little boy being brought up by his father or mother to look at the procession as we pass by, I think of you and Archie and feel very homesick. Sometimes little boys ride in the procession on their ponies, just like Archie on Algonquin.

Letters regarding the trip extended beyond the actual travel. Writing to Senator Henry Cabot Lodge on June 6, 1903, describing the badger he had brought home to the White House, the president said, "Josiah, the young badger, is hailed with the wildest enthusiasm by the children, and has passed an affectionate but passionate day with us. Fortunately his temper seems proof." While Roosevelt was writing letters, so was John Muir. On May 10, he sent this missive to his friend, the journalist F. Bailey Millard:

Dear Mr. Millard:

I have been hoping that I would have a quiet ceanothus day with you at your Tamalpais home before starting on my long trip, and the girls hoped to join me. But many small time-consuming cares have held me here. Can you meet me at Keith's studio about 12 o' clock next Wednesday and go out to lunch with me? If not please tell me where I can meet you for a goodbye word.

I leave the city with the President's Yosemite party about midnight May 14th.

With best wishes to all your family, I am

Sincerely Yours,
John Muir

The next day, President Roosevelt arrived in Santa Cruz (he also visited Watsonville and Pajaro); included was a special visit to the redwood grove there, today called the Henry Cowell Redwoods. Just before making his way from the beach city up into the mountains to see the famous giants, he gave this speech:

I am about to visit the grove of the great trees. I wish to congratulate you people of California, people of this region, and to congratulate all the country on what you have done in preserving these great trees. Cut down one of these giants and you cannot fill its place. The ages were their architects and we owe it to ourselves and to our children's children to preserve them. Nothing has pleased me more here in California than to see how thoroughly awake you are to preserve the monuments of the past, human and natural. I am glad to see the way in which the old mission buildings are being preserved. This great, wonderful, new State, this State which is itself an empire, situated on the greatest of oceans, should keep alive the sense of historic continuity of its past, and should as one step towards that end preserve the ancient historic landmarks within its limits. I am even more pleased that you should be preserving the great and wonderful natural features here, that you should have in California a park like the Yosemite, that we should have State preserves of these great trees and other preserves where individuals and associations have kept them. We should see to it that no man for speculative purposes or for mere temporary use exploits the groves of great trees. Where the individuals and associations of individuals cannot preserve them, the State, and, if necessary, the nation, should step in and see to their preservation. We should keep the trees as we should keep great stretches of the wildernesses as a heritage for our children and our children's children. Our aim should be to preserve them for use, to preserve them for beauty, for the sake of the nation hereafter.

The nation's chief before the forest king—President Roosevelt in Big Tree Grove, Santa Cruz, California.

I shall not try to make any extended address to you. I shall only say how glad I am to be here, bid you welcome with all my heart, and say how thoroughly I believe in you, and that I am a better American for being among you.

Once arriving at the majestic grove, he was appalled to see calling cards and advertising posters pinned into their soft bark. His speech reflects his anger:

Mr. Mayor, and Ladies First, and to the Rest of the Guests in the Second Place: I want to thank you very much for your courtesy in receiving me, and to say how much I have enjoyed being here. This is the first glimpse I have ever had of the big trees, and I wish to pay the highest tribute I can to the State of California, to those private citizens and associations of citizens who have co-operated with the State in preserving these wonderful trees for the whole nation, in preserving them in whatever part of the State they may be found. All of us ought to want to see nature preserved; and take a big tree whose architect has been the ages, anything that man does toward it may

The flower-covered engine drawing President Roosevelt's special train in Santa Cruz, California.

President Roosevelt plants a tree near San Jose, California.

hurt it and cannot help it; and above all, the rash creature who wishes to leave his name to mar the beauties of nature should be sternly discouraged. Take those cards pinned up on that tree; they give an air of the ridiculous to this solemn and majestic grove. (Applause) To pin those cards up there is as much out of place as if you tacked so many tin cans up there. I mean that literally. You should save the people whose names are there from the reprobation of every individual by taking down the cards at the earliest possible moment; and do keep these trees, keep all the wonderful scenery of this wonderful State unmarred by the vandalism or the folly of man. Remember that we have to contend not merely with knavery, but with folly;

and see to it that you by your actions create the kind of public opinion which will put a stop to any destruction of or any marring of the wonderful and beautiful gifts that you have received from nature, that you ought to hand on as a precious heritage to your children and your children's children. I am, oh, so glad to be here, to be in this majestic and beautiful grove, to see the wonderful redwoods, and I thank you for giving me the chance, and I do hope that it will be your object to preserve them as nature made them and left them, for the future.

After speaking, and refusing an official escort, Roosevelt next went to cool off in a nearby grove. When he returned, the cards had been taken down.

On the morning of May 13, in San Francisco, the president was escorted by a squadron of cavalry through streets lined with people to Native Sons Hall, where a reception was held. The hall was packed with members of the California Society of Pioneers, the Native Sons of the Golden West, the Native Daughters and veterans of the Mexican-American War.

Next the president proceeded to Van Ness Avenue, where thousands of schoolchildren had assembled, many of them carrying beautiful silk banners and all of them having flags, which were waved as the president passed. After the review of the children, he drove to the Presidio and then to the golf links, where there was a military review, General MacArthur being in command of the troops. Today there is rare film footage of the president passing the schoolchildren along the city streets. A bay area newspaper recounted part of the visit:

Roosevelt riding in a parade in San Francisco on May 13.

Roosevelt delivering the University of California–Berkeley commencement speech on May 14.

After a drive through Golden Gate Park, luncheon was taken at the Cliff House, with the members of the executive committee, Gov. Pardee, Adm. Bickford and other invited guests. On the return trip, a large crowd witnessed the president turn the first shovelful of earth for the McKinley Monument. The shovel was a souvenir one, made from the material of which the monument will be composed, and it was presented to the president. In a brief address he said: "It is not too much to say that no man since Lincoln was as widely, universally loved in this country as was Pres. McKinley, for it was given to him, not only to rise to the most exalted station, but to typify in his character and conduct those virtues which every American citizen worthy of the name like to regard as typically American—the virtues of cleanly and upright living, in all relations, private and public, and the most intimate family relations, and

Roosevelt delivers a speech in Berkeley, California. *Theodore Roosevelt Collection, Houghton Library, Harvard University.*

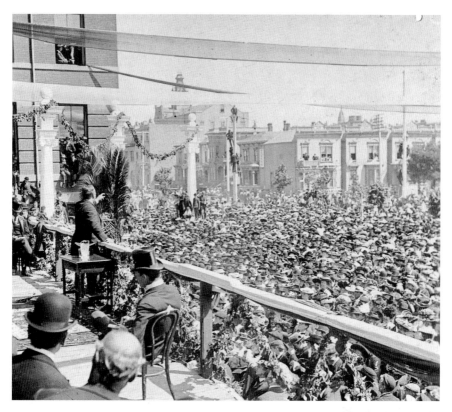

Roosevelt delivers a speech in Oakland, California, on Thursday, May 14. The next day, he would travel to Yosemite.

the relations of business, and relations with his neighbors, and finally in his conduct of the great affairs of state.

That evening, the president spoke at the mechanics pavilion, with the subject being expansion and trade development and protection of the country's newly acquired possessions in the Pacific.

On the morning of May 14, the president participated in the dedication of the monument to the victory of Commodore Dewey and his fleet in Manila Bay. The monument still stands today. The president then went to Berkeley, where he took part in the commencement exercises of the University of California, with President Benjamin Ide Wheeler conferring on him the degree of Doctor of Laws.

Another image of Roosevelt delivering the University of California–Berkeley commencement speech on May 14.

After visiting Oakland, where the citizens cordially greeted him, the president laid the cornerstone of the Navy YMCA. In the evening, he was given a farewell banquet by the Union League Club at the Palace Hotel. And then it was time to meet John Muir.

Chapter 5
LET THE REAL ADVENTURE BEGIN

Yosemite

Linnie Marsh Wolfe's exquisite 1945 biography, *Son of the Wilderness: The Life of John Muir*, described the tension that John Muir felt in having to delay a trip with the professor Charles Sargent in order to accommodate Roosevelt:

> *Muir was torn between two loyalties—his duty to the trees, and his promise, long since given, to start at that time with Sargent on a world tour. The president learning of his dilemma, wrote him an urgent personal message: "I do not want anyone with me but you, and I want to drop politics absolutely for four days, and just be out in the open with you." So Muir put the problem up to Sargent saying "An influential man from Washington wants to make a trip to the Sierra with me, and I might be able to do some forest good and talking freely around the campfire." Sargent of course, postponed the date of sailing. But being a stickler for dates and schedules, he applied certain adjectives of the blankety-blank sort to Roosevelt.*
>
> *On the appointed day the president arrived in San Francisco, and "the city that knows how" turned out with dramatic fanfare to honor him. On the night of the 14th, while he was being fêted at the Palace Hotel, Muir came down to join the party for an early start the next morning. Arthur Coleman, his business manager, came with him, and joining F. Bailey Millard, the journalist, they all walked up Market Street. Muir, bewildered by the tumult and glare, soon declared he was tired and wanted to go to bed. Coleman protested that since he was the president's guest, he should wait*

up for him. Muir shook his head, saying that not for a president or any man would he lose sleep. So returning over the ferry to the Oakland Mole, with the presidential train waiting, he went straight to his berth. Millard, commenting upon this incident said: "This seems a bit strange, but if you knew John Muir, you would know that it was the most likely think he could have done. Pose? Not a bit of it. He is as incapable of pose as a grizzly and about as hard to tackle if you go at him the wrong way."

In the morning after breakfast he went into the president's car to meet his host. In the course of their very cordial conversation he pulled Sargent's letter from his pocket and, forgetting the blankety-blank adjectives, handed it over to Roosevelt to read. But nothing could ruffle the good humor of T.R. that morning. He fairly howled over the opprobrious words, and Muir's embarrassment, as he grabbed a letter back only increased the president's query. He seems truly to have borne no ill will since he provided travelers with a letter that brought them many courtesies abroad.

That morning, May 15, the men first met in what would have been the small town of Raymond, California. From 1886 until the completion of the Yosemite Valley Railroad in 1907, the closest a traveler could get to Yosemite by train was the town of Raymond, located in the foothills of Madera County. From here, a stagecoach ride was required.

Today, the train station at Raymond is long gone, but a piece of the original track has been preserved. The president's car rolled over these. The Bowen Hotel, where Roosevelt gave a short speech, is also gone. It's a quiet little place today, but the morning Roosevelt and company rolled up, it was a bustle of activity. In 1933, Raymond resident Archibald Campbell Shaw wrote an account for the *Raymond Tattler*:

In May 1903, President Roosevelt visited California, the Yosemite Valley and Raymond. The residents of Raymond planned a big celebration in his honor. A band and an orchestra were enlarged; a dance platform built, races and games planned. Raymond was the only stop Roosevelt made between San Francisco and Yosemite at which he spoke. With him on the trip were John Muir, Governor Pardee and his staff. When the President's special pulled into Raymond depot at about 8 A.M.—there were assembled about fifteen hundred people to greet him. The reception committee, James Marner, Dr. Topp and myself met the President as he was about to leave his car. When requested to speak, he said that he had no notice of the meeting and would have to change his outing (khaki) clothes to a more conventional suit.

However upon the committee's insistence he addressed the crowd, as he was, from a platform made ready on P.M. Bowen's store porch.

The writer had the honor and pleasure of introducing to the largest audience ever assembled in Raymond, the President of the United States, Theodore Roosevelt! Neither time nor space permits narration of the detail of the President's trip but outstanding was his pleasure in seeing Yosemite with John Muir, with Archie Leonard as guide and Charles Leidig as cook—going in on horseback from the Mariposa Big Trees with them, and sending the rest of the party in by stage.

Writer and Yosemite history expert Hank Johnston wrote a wonderful 1994 article in Yosemite magazine which also included details of the president's arrival in Raymond, and where he was headed. The necessary arrangements followed, and at 7:30 on the morning of May 15, 1903, having traveled overnight from Oakland, the presidential special train pulled into Raymond station, the nearest mainline rail connection to Yosemite, with Muir and Roosevelt on board. According to witnesses, a band was playing, bunting and flags waved from every building, and more

The only known photograph of Theodore Roosevelt making his impromptu speech in the town of Raymond in front of the Bowen Hotel.

than 1000 cheering spectators were assembled in eager anticipation of the president's arrival. Somewhat disconcerted by the unexpected attention, Roosevelt, dressed informally in Norfolk coat, baggy breeches, leather leggings, no purchase, and nondescript sombrero, briefly [addressed] *the crowd from the veranda of the Bowen hotel before entering the first of 211 passenger stages that were waiting to transport him and his entourage to the Mariposa Grove of big trees. The president sat in the front seat of the lead vehicle beside veteran Yosemite stage and turnpike company driver Bright Gillespie. Muir sat directly behind Roosevelt so he could point out places of interest. They were joined by the remaining members of the official party: Sec. of the Navy William H Moody; California Gov. George C Pardee; Dr. Presley and Rick C, Surgeon General; Nicholas Murray Butler, president of Columbia University; Roosevelt's private secretary William Loeb Junior; and Benjamin Ide Wheeler. The second stage, which followed a short distance behind, carried four Secret Service agents and various other attendents. Accompanying the stages was a crack detachment of 30 US cavalry men, mounted on matching dappled gray horses, commanded by a Lieutenant Mays.*

After the customary lunch stop at the Wawona Hotel, 18 miles above Raymond, the party proceeded directly to the Mariposa Grove of big trees. Here, following some preliminaries such as picture taking at the grizzly giant and Wawona tunnel tree, the president dismissed the troops thanking them for their services and calling out as they departed, God bless you. He also sent away the press and photographers, who fully expected Roosevelt to rejoin them later at the bedecked Wawona Hotel where a lavish banquet scheduled for 6 PM. The president then bade a temporary goodbye to the members of his party who, except for Muir, boarded the stage and headed for the sanctuary of the hotel 6 miles away.

This was the president's speech in Raymond, in front of the Bowen Hotel:

Mr. Chairman, Ladies and Gentlemen: I did not realize that I was to meet you today, still less to address an audience such as this and I had only come prepared to go into the Yosemite with John Muir, so I must ask you to excuse my costume. (Cries of, "It is all right!") I have enjoyed so much seeing Southern California and San Francisco that I felt my trip would be incomplete if I did not get up into your beautiful country and then see the Yosemite. Before I came on this trip I was inclined to grumble because I found we were giving relatively four times as much time to California as to any other State. Now I feel that we did not give it half enough. It ought to have been eight times instead of four times. I have enjoyed being here. I have never been on the Pacific Coast before. For a number of years I lived in the Rockies. I was in the cow business in those days. Great though my pleasure has been in seeing your wonderful soil, your wonderful climate, your fruits and flowers, your extraordinary and beautiful natural products, yet what I have liked most has been meeting the men and women, and finding that the fundamental fact throughout this country is that wherever you go, from the Atlantic to the Pacific, a good American is a good American, and nothing else. (Applause) Here, as everywhere that I have been in California, I am greeted by men who wear the button which shows that in the times that tried men's souls they proved their truth by their endeavor. As they then belonged to different regiments, doubtless raised in different States, but fought for one flag and one country, so now wherever we are citizens, in the East, in the West, or here beyond the West, in California, wherever we are citizens, our duties are the same; our duty is to lead our lives in a spirit of decency, of courage and of common sense, that will make us fit to be citizens of this great republic.

The adventure was officially on. From here, night one would be spent at the Mariposa Grove of sequoia trees, night two would be high above at Glacier Point and, finally, night three would be in the valley at Bridalveil Fall. Newspapers were agog with president's sense of adventure, breathlessly reporting details for the entire country to enjoy. This was a wire report from May 16, 1903:

Pres. Roosevelt, for the second time since he left Washington on his present trip, is cut off from communication with the outside world. He is camping in the big tree country and will remain secluded until Monday morning. His special train arrived at Raymond early in the morning. A detachment of the ninth cavalry, which is stationed at Wawona, was at the station to meet him and act as an escort in the big tree country.

As soon as the president had finished breakfast he left his car and made a short speech to the large crowd that had collected. He thanked them for greeting him and mentioned the good time he expected to have during his four days stay in the Yosemite Valley. The president and his party then boarded stages and started on the 40-mile ride to the big tree country, where the night was spent.

Luncheon was eaten at the Wawona Hotel, which his stage reached in record time. An exciting incident occurred during the ride from Wawona to the big tree Grove. A small forest fire was raging close to the trail, causing

Early on the morning of Sunday, May 17, 1903. Theodore Roosevelt (left) and John Muir pose at Glacier Point after having spent the night camping nearby.

a heavy pall of smoke to obscure the road. The trail at this place runs along the steep side of the mountain. The driver lashed the horses, and the president was soon out of the fire zone. It was about 4:00 PM when the party reached the Big Tree Grove, and the president spent two hours admiring these wonders of nature. He then mounted a horse and with John Muir, the naturalist, and guides Leonard and Leidig, members of the forest rangers, started for camp.

President Roosevelt amid nature's wonders, driving through the famous "Tunnel Tree" located at the Mariposa Grove at Yosemite.

Another account from May 16 reported on the monumental adventure:

President Roosevelt has not been heard from today. He is supposed to have been in the vicinity of Glacier Point this morning and is thought to be at the hotel tonight, but there was no word from him to Secretary Loeb when his party reached the Sentinel hotel here this afternoon.

Snow fell today in the mountains in which the president is traveling and the weather became quite cold. Should the weather become too cold for outdoor camping there are a number of shanties located in different parts of the mountains in which the president could spend the night quite comfortably. Notwithstanding the fact that the president, before leaving Washington, outlined the program he was to follow during his stay in

President Theodore Roosevelt poses at Glacier Point early on the morning of Sunday, May 17, 1903.

PRESIDENT LEAVES FAMOUS YOSEMITE

Nation's Chief Resumes His Tour by Train After His Rapturous Outing in the Suns and Snows of the Incomparable Valley

BEAUTIFUL FALLING WATERS IN YOSEMITE VALLEY, NEAR WHICH PRESIDENT ROOSEVELT MADE HIS CAMP WITH JOHN MUIR ON ONE OF THE NIGHTS DURING HIS OUTING.

One of the many dramatic newspaper accounts of the president's visit to Yosemite.

the assembly, the assembly park commission decided that he should follow another program, which they adopted without consulting him. This latter program provided for fireworks, the firing of dynamite to produce loud echoes and the participation by the president in some sort of public ceremony.

Without the president's knowledge this program was circulated broadcast and people came in the Yosemite from hundreds of miles away to see him. When they found that the president was not to be seen the disappointment was very great. The president was not told of this proposed change in the program until yesterday and even then he was not told the people were coming from such long distances to see him. As he was tired out as the result of the hospitality of San Francisco he decided that he would adhere to the original plan and spend the next few days in seclusion. Jorgenson's cabin, in the center of the valley is well-prepared for the president and he's eagerly awaited. All the hotels in public camps are crowded overflowing. [The "Jorgensen" referred to was Chris Jorgensen, the noted painter who lived in the valley and whose cabin had been prepared for Roosevelt to spend a night. However, Roosevelt opted to not interrupt his camping plans.]

Here was yet another article, which had been picked up by the *San Francisco Chronicle*:

The president camped in the Mariposa Big Tree Grove last night. He and Mr. Muir were up at dawn this morning. They came tearing down Lightning Trail, one of the steepest trails in the mountains and passed the hotel at an early hour on a fast gallop. The president looked very buoyant as he rode by, but did not look to the right and left. Only a few people were up early enough to see them go by.

The plans of camping are still kept secret, but it is supposed he will camp somewhere in the vicinity of Glacier Point. There is a great amount of snow on the Glacier Point Road. Washburn Brothers sent a man out on the road a week ago to break a trail in for the president's use. In some places they reported the snow was 14 feet deep. Today the weather changed and became very cold. It is feared that it is snowing in the glacial meadows. Plenty of blankets and a good shelter tent provided by the Yosemite Stage and Turnpike Company means that even if it does snow, the president will be very comfortable. Some in his party say that this is just the kind of trip he'll enjoy. Severe weather cannot frighten him. If he makes Glacier Point tonight he will have covered 35 miles of the hardest kind of mountain climbing.

Tomorrow night, it is thought, he will camp in Little Yosemite. Mr. Muir is making the itinerary and as he discovered the Little Yosemite, it is likely he will go there. Those are excellent camping grounds and fine fishing. Monday morning the president will come down the Vernal and Nevada Falls trails and gallop down the valley to the Bridalveil, a distance of 6½ miles, where he will meet his stage leaving

Another of the splashy front-page accounts of Roosevelt's adventure.

the valley. It is thought that he will not stop at the lower hotel at all, as he said on leaving that he did not want to step inside of a hotel for three days.

The assembly commissioners and people in the Valley are sorely disappointed that the president is not going to make them a visit. They have decorated the valley profusely and had arranged a lengthy program, but the president said he was tired of electric lights, bombs, etc. and that he intended to enjoy himself up here. His sole guide for this trip is Muir and when anyone asked him what was going to be done he referred them to Muir. Several itineraries were arranged for him, but Muir had arranged an entirely different one. Secretary Loeb was the only man in his party that knew of the proposed plans. A good many of the party remained over at the Wawona and do not intend on visiting the valley at all. They claim the beauties of Wawona will satisfy them and since the president is not going to be in the valley they prefer to remain here and join him on his way down. When the president finishes his trip he will be thoroughly familiar with Yosemite National Park, besides having seen Glacier Point, Vernal and Nevada Falls and having had a ride down the floor of the valley. He will see as much of the assembly as the ordinary tourists. His time will not be taken up by speechmaking, but instead by sightseeing. The president was very much pleased with the courtesies of the stage company in passing his party. Nothing was lacking in making the trip as pleasant as possible and in the quickest time.

The *Chronicle* continued its intense reporting. This piece ran in May 1903:

"Roosevelt Pitches His Camp Near Bleak Sentinel Dome in Snowstorm"

There were no dusty roads for Pres. Roosevelt or his attendants today. Instead of the shelter of the great spreading trees, the warm sunshine and the singing birds, the president rode through the deep snow, accompanied by John Muir and guides Leonard and Leidig, stopping now and then to allow their fatigued horses to rest before plunging through another snowdrift. Occasionally they would throw their bridle reins over the pommels and turn partly around in their saddles to view some gigantic cliff or tortuous valley that spread off to one side of the difficult trail, which they were traveling.

The start was made early in the morning from the big trees, where the presidents bivouac had been made the night before. The president rose greatly refreshed, the sleep in the clear, cool air of the mountains having greatly relieved his fatigue of the previous day's hard trip. He was anxious to be off with as little delay as possible, and so no stop was made at the Wawona hotel, where the remainder of his party, consisting of private secretary Loeb, Gov. Pardee, Benjamin Ide Wheeler and others had spent the night.

Avoiding the main road, and long before most of his associates were up, the president, filled with his usual enthusiasm for adventure, passed rapidly down the narrow defile known as Lightning Trail and struck off for the Yosemite Valley. An hour later the main road was reached and the steep ascent to the top of Chinquapin began. The party reached the summit before noon, and then the difficult portion of the trip began. Here the party not only had the steepest ascents, but the deep snow as well. Slowly they passed by Crescent Lake, Bucks Camp and Ostrader Lake, reaching Mono Meadows about 2 o'clock. Here the steep grades were left behind and the rest of the trip to Glacier Point was made with only the deep snow to contend with. About 4 miles from the point the president passed Dewey Trail, named in honor of Adm. Dewey and which leads over to the top of Bridalveil Fall.

Late in the afternoon, the president, rather worn and weary with his hard day's march, reached the heights at the back of Glacier Point, and his camp was pitched just back of Sentinel Dome. During all of the afternoon the party worked their way over a difficult defile, struggling to see their narrow trail in the midst of a blinding snowstorm. For three weeks the weather conditions around the valley had been perfect, but today a change took place as the warm sunshine of the previous days gave way to overcast skies and whirling snow. In the valley itself the snow changed to rain, drenching the members of the presidential party as they proceeded up the difficult heights of the Glacier Point trail.

Again tonight the president and his faithful guides will sleep in the wilderness listening to the sigh of the pine boughs as they swing in the night breezes that blow over the heights of Glacier and Signal peaks, 7000 feet above sea level. Should the storm increase in violence tonight the president and his escort will make their way to the Glacier Point hotel, located some 3 miles away.

Tomorrow the itinerary will probably consist of the trip to the 3000 feet precipice of Glacier Point and a circular journey of 14 miles past Vernal and Nevada Falls and Happy Isles to the valley. The president today seems inclined to express his regrets to Mr. Jorgensen for his kind offer of hospitality and instead of occupying his picturesque cabin, take a tent on the floor of the valley tomorrow night. He says he wishes to rough it on this trip, as he has done so many times in the mountains of Colorado.

This illustration was created by the artist Charles Lewis Bartholomew. It was described at the time as a "glimpse of how the President has been spending his time the past few days, sight unseen. Theodore Roosevelt in hiking gear, flying through the air near El Capitan in Yosemite."

Gov. Pardee and Sec. Loeb led the vanguard out of the Wawona and were followed by five stage leads consisting of the other members of the president's party. The start was made without any unusual incidents at 7 o'clock and the party arrived at Chinquapin about two hours behind the president and his guides. From there the road was downgrade until Inspiration Point was reached, where most of the party caught their first glimpse of the beautiful valley reposing peacefully in the distance before them. Here a brief stop was made by the drivers until the party could drink in a few of the details that made up the picturesque scene. Benjamin Ide Wheeler thought the valley superior to anything around his university campus; Gov. Pardee said it was a scene worthy of the state that owned it, and Sec. Loeb admitted that it equals anything yet ever seen.

A pause was also made of Bridalveil Fall, with 600 feet of falling water viewed, and then the party proceeded to the entrance to the valley that is guarded so royally by mighty El Capitan and the lofty cathedral rocks. The next stop was made of the Sentinel Hotel, where the members were assigned quarters by J.B. Cook, the proprietor. A little later the party, with the exception of Governor Pardee, who decided to remain in the valley, again took seats in the stages and were driven rapidly over to the foot of Glacier Trail, where the ascent was immediately begun to the heights above.

This is how the *San Francisco Chronicle* covered the final night of the camping trip at Yosemite trip on May 17:

President Roosevelt, John Muir and Rangers Charles Leidig and Archie Leonard are encamped in the Veil Meadows tonight. Near the banks of the Merced, in a grove of pines and firs, almost within the spray of the beautiful Bridalveil Fall, the chief executive is resting after one of the most memorable day trips of his life. At 3 o'clock this afternoon the party arrived from Vernal Falls at the bridge over the Merced, at the Happy Isles. Although they had been hovering above the Yosemite since early morning, first at the heights of Glacier Point, then above the great panorama wall near the Vernal Falls and later at the Nevada and Vernal Falls, yet this was their first entrance to the floor of the valley. There were but few there to meet him because his point of entrance was not known to anyone, not even the members of his party he spoke kindly to there and then came down the valley via Camp Curry and to the Sentinel Lodge.

It was not known on just what road or trail the party would come down the valley and so several went over to the Yosemite Falls to possibly get a glimpse of him. A wheelman, however, came down from Camp Curry and reported that the president was coming down the regular road. Shortly before 4 o'clock the party was seen approaching the Sentinel. A few minutes later they had arrived at the hotel and in front of the bridge and arch. Upon the latter in large moss covered letters with the words, "Welcome to Yosemite." The president was greeted by Pres. Wheeler and others. He then alighted and for a few minutes he spoke pleasantly to a few members of his party.

PLEASED WITH THE STORM

"We were in a snowstorm last night and it was just what I wanted," said he smiling. He was dressed in a khaki suit, Army hat and around his neck was a dusty looking handkerchief, much the worse for wear.

In a few minutes he mounted his horse, passing under the arch and crossed the bridge. On the north side he again alighted, and with John Muir and Pres. Wheeler, proceeded to the Jorgensen studio 200 feet up the river, being joined by Mr. Jorgensen. This building has the honor of being the only one he was in while here. They remained there for over half hour and the president expressed himself fully about the Yosemite and the Sierras.

A big lunch was awaiting him and caterer Johnson of the Bohemian club was on hand to do the honors. Though his appetite was keen, he refused to eat, having in mind the camp meal at the Bridalveil Meadows. However, he joined the party in a glass of wine.

"This is one day of my life," said he, "and one that I will always remember with pleasure. Just think of where I was last night. Up there," pointing toward Glacier Point, "amid the Pines and silver firs, in the Sierran solitude in a snowstorm, too, and without a tent. I passed one of the most pleasant nights of my life. It was so reviving to be so close to nature in this magnificent forest of yours."

He said much more than this and he meant it, too. Then they showed him through all the rooms of the studio. "Had I not wanted the complete rest that I have had it would have been one of the greatest pleasures of my life to have spent time in this building," said he.

When they showed him the dining hall with its beautiful Dutch finish and furniture his eyes fairly glistened and he said, "You know, I am Dutch myself."

In the meantime a large party had assembled at the end of the bridge. It was quiet and orderly. When he came out of the studio, accompanied by the others of the party, he walked quietly back to the bridge and then held an informal reception [that lasted] 10 minutes or more. The key of the valley, made of Manzanita by Julius Stare was given him by Guardian Stevens. "Here is a good Republican," said the Democrat, presenting his wife.

The president smiled and warmly greeted both. A little baby was brought to him in his father's arms. He shook its tiny hand and with a merry twinkle said, "I have a half dozen myself."

A former member of the seventh infantry named McPherson, who was close to the Roughriders in Cuba, was warmly greeted and for a moment the beauties of Yosemite were lost sight of and the stormy days of the charge up the hills near Santiago were recalled and discussed. He shook hands with all and warmly greeted them. He felt perfectly at home and the people felt that they were greeting an old friend. Cameras and Kodak's were snapping on all sides. As the president re-crossed the bridge three cheers were given him. Then he passed under the arch and rode, unaccompanied by anyone, down the street of Yosemite Village. A small boy said "Hello Teddy!" The president stopped his horse and a frown darkened his face. He rode up to the boy, the dignity of the president gone and in its place the face and severity of the father and parent. He gave that youngster a short lecture on manners that he will never forget.

Several times he stopped to greet someone or answer a salutation and then disappeared in the pine-lined road that leads down to the camping place, for the night. About 2 miles below town he was met by a party consisting of Gov. Pardee, Judge Henshaw and Yosemite commissioners Givens and Henshaw. It was a purely informal and unexpected meeting and much enjoyed by all.

Tomorrow morning the president will take the Raymond Limited Stage at 6 o'clock, lunch at Wawona and arrive at Raymond in the evening, where his special train awaits him. For two days and two nights he has been lost to the world and its curious gaping crowd and the almost trackless wilds of the high sierras, accompanied by John Muir and forest rangers Leidig and Leonard. Muir knows all about the animals in the mountains, and the president can ask questions.

When he reached the Mariposa Grove of big trees Friday evening the president was a tired, worried man. This evening he is bright, alert, the Roosevelt of old. Human-like he lay upon the soil under the great sequoias and rested. "Will see you gentlemen Monday," said he, and then, after posing at the foot of the grizzly giant for a photograph, he went to the camp of the rangers nearby.

At an early hour yesterday morning they were up and on their way to Yosemite. They avoided, however, all roads except at Wawona, where they were compelled to cross the South Fork of the Merced on the bridge. The people at the hotel expected them to come from big trees so as to pass in front of the hotel. But the rangers knew the country, and they hugged the riverbank so closely that they passed to the east of the hotel without being seen, though within 100 yards of the place.

Then they left the road and followed an old Indian trail leading to glacier point. During most of the day the two rangers headed the party, followed by the president and Muir. At different times they got into as much as 7 feet of snow, but these were only patches. They had more trouble with the muddy meadows than with the snow. One of the pleasant events of the day was their seeing 17 deer. Though there are bear in these parts they did not see any.

SHAVING AND SNOW

Last night they camped about a mile back from the rim of the Yosemite, retiring in about 10 o'clock. A real but short Sierran snowstorm was on for a short time during the evening, but did not annoy the president. He shaved himself by the light of the great campfire while the snowflakes were falling. Breakfast at camp was over at 6:15 o'clock this morning, and then he and Muir walked over to Glacier Point. There they remained nearly an hour. From the supernatural heights of Glacier Point, nearly a mile above the floor of Yosemite, the president saw the wonders of the valley. And to the east and west and northeast of the great granite gorges of the high seers, snow mantled and glistened in the rays of the early morning sun. The late Prof. Whitney said that this was the greatest view on earth.

Above: Roosevelt at Washburn Point, near Glacier Point, on the morning of Sunday, May 17, 1903.

Opposite: Photograph showing Roosevelt and seven other men seated in a horse-drawn carriage at Inspiration Point in Yosemite Valley, California. Roosevelt is second from the far right, and naturalist John Muir is seated behind him out of view.

They arrived in the Little Yosemite at noon and lunched there, the president lying upon the ground for some time and sleeping. Hot coffee was made, the other part of the lunch having been prepared in the morning. From that time until they reach the floor of the valley at the Happy Isles, as noted above, they visited both the Nevada and the Vernal Falls.

There was no order today. Sometimes the president was in the rear, at others in front. He was like a schoolboy—happy. He told Ranger Leidig that he soon will be a better cook than the chef of the Palace Hotel. At meals he helped himself and when his saddle needed recinching he did not call a ranger, but attended to it himself. When some people on horses started to follow his party from the Happy Isles he wrote his side and asked them to ride on in front. "I do not like to lead a procession" he said to them.

[In his own autobiography, Roosevelt wrote this about the trip:] When I first visited California, it was my good fortune to see the "big trees," the Sequoias, and then to travel down into the Yosemite, with John Muir. Of course of all people in the world he was the one with whom it was best worthwhile thus to see the Yosemite. He told me that when Emerson came to California he tried to get him to come out and camp with him, for that was the only way in which to see at their best the majesty and charm of the Sierras. But at the time Emerson was getting old and could not go.

John Muir met me with a couple of packers and two mules to carry our tent, bedding, and food for a three days' trip. The first night was clear, and we lay down in the darkening aisles of the great Sequoia grove. The majestic trunks, beautiful in color and in symmetry, rose round us like the pillars of a mightier cathedral than ever was conceived even by the fervor of the Middle Ages. Hermit thrushes sang beautifully in the evening, and again, with a burst of wonderful music, at dawn.

I was interested and a little surprised to find that, unlike John Burroughs, John Muir cared little for birds or bird songs, and knew little about them. The hermit-thrushes meant nothing to him, the trees and the flowers and the cliffs everything. The only birds he noticed or cared for were some that were very conspicuous, such as the water-ouzels, always particular favorites of mine too. The second night we camped in a snow-storm, on the edge of the cañon walls, under the spreading limbs of a grove of mighty silver fir; and next day we went down into the wonderland of the valley itself. I shall always be glad that I was in the Yosemite with John Muir and in the Yellowstone with John Burroughs.

One of the men who led Roosevelt on the trip, ranger Charles Leidig, recorded his own thoughts on the trip. His recollections were filed in the Yosemite Research Library:

Charlie Leidig stated that John Muir and Abner Mann, who had a travel office at the Palace Hotel in San Francisco for the Yosemite Stage and Turnpike Co, arranged that Archie Leonard and he were to be guides and escorts for Theodore Roosevelt. Muir came from San Francisco on the train with the presidential party of eight, including Governor George C. Pardee of California, Benjamin Ide Wheeler, president of the University of California, and Roosevelt's personal secretary Mr. Loeb. The group was placed in an eleven-passenger coach of which Bright Gulispe was the driver. Under Lieutenant Mays, thirty cavalrymen escorted this stage from Raymond directly to the Grizzly Giant in the Mariposa Grove. There, the party was photographed especially by Underwood and Underwood. Leidig and Leonard were not in the picture.

After some preliminaries, President Roosevelt dismissed the troops, thanking them for their services and calling out after them as they departed, "God bless you." The stage departed with all members of the president's party, except Mr. Roosevelt, John Muir, Charlie Leidig, Archie Leonard, and an Army packer named Jacher Alder. The president said to Charlie Leidig, "Leidig, please do not let anybody disturb me, because I am tired and want rest and sleep." Charlie did the cooking. He said they had fried chicken and beefsteak for supper that night. The president drank strong, black coffee and went to bed early under the Grizzly Giant.

The only cover provided for the president was a "shelter half" under which about forty blankets were piled to serve as a bed. The president got just as deep into these as he wanted for warmth and comfort. Four mules were used to haul this gear. On May 16, 1903, the group broke camp at the Mariposa Grove and were on horses by 6:30 a.m. The president directed Leidig to "outskirt and keep away from civilization." Leidig led the party down the Lightning Trail. They crossed the South Fork at Greeley's and hit the Empire Meadows Trail. They especially avoided approaching the Wawona Hotel for fear the president would be brought in contact with members of his own official party, which had remained for the night in Wawona. They had a cold lunch on the ridge east of Empire Meadows. There was lots of snow as they crossed towards Sentinel Dome; they took turns breaking trail through deep snow. In the Bridal Veil Meadows the party plowed through five feet of snow.

Riding in Yosemite. *From left to right:* guide Archie Leonard, John Muir, Roosevelt and guide Charles Leidig.

The president mired down, and Charlie had to get a log to get him out. It was snowing hard and the wind was blowing. Muir proposed that they camp on the ridge just back of Sentinel Dome. Leidig's suggestion, however, that they travel down to the approximate location of existing campgrounds at Glacier Point, where water and better camping conditions in May could be found, prevailed. It snowed five inches during that night and everything was frozen in the morning. Leidig remembered that around the campfire that night Roosevelt and Muir talked far into the night regarding Muir's glacial theory of the formation of Yosemite Valley. They talked a great deal about the conservation of forests in general and Yosemite in particular, and discussed the setting aside of other areas in the United States for park purposes. Leidig recounted that during the trip Muir seemed to bother the president by picking twigs for Roosevelt's buttonhole. He noted that some difficulty was encountered because both men wanted to do the talking. On the morning of May 16, the party went down to Glacier Point for pictures that had been prearranged. As they left Glacier Point, the president rode in front followed by Leidig, Leonard, Muir, and the packer. They were all dressed in civilian attire. The rangers wore blue overalls, chaps, and spurs. They rode into Little Yosemite Valley for lunch, where they encountered a considerable crowd of valley visitors, since it had been widely advertised in the papers that the president was visiting the park. Leidig observed that many times during the trip President Roosevelt demonstrated his great love for birds by whistling, and the birds, many of which he was able to identify, would answer him. There was considerable disagreement in the matter of plans for the presidential visit.

Roosevelt wanted a roughing trip, and through Pardee, Wheeler, and Muir, such a trip had been worked out. On the other hand, John Stevens, Guardian of the Yosemite Grant under state administration, and certain of the commissioners, especially Jack Wilson of San Francisco, had made plans for a large celebration. The Chris Jorgensen studio home had been set aside for the president's official use. A cook had been engaged from one of the best hotels in San Francisco to serve a banquet. The commissioners had arranged a considerable display of fireworks, which John Degnan claimed amounted to some $1,800 worth.

Degnan said he was to have had some part in touching this off for the president's benefit. So there were a number of people awaiting the president at the top of Nevada Falls and in Little Yosemite Valley. Roosevelt requested that everyone be kept at a distance in order that he could carry out his desire for a "roughing trip"; accordingly the collected crowd was kept away from the presidential party. When the group reached Camp Curry at 2 p.m., they found a big crowd of women in front of the camp. They had formed a big line across the road in an attempt to stop the president. They all wanted to shake hands with him. Leidig was riding second in line carrying a Winchester rifle and six-shooter. His horse was a high-spirited animal. Roosevelt said, "I am very much annoyed, couldn't you do something?" Leidig replied, "Follow me." He gave spurs to his horse, and as he reared, women fell apart and the president's party went through the gap. Roosevelt waved his hat to the group as he headed off down the road. At Sentinel Bridge, the guardian of the valley and some of the commissioners assembled with members of the presidential party to meet Roosevelt. The president dismounted, clearly tired, and Charlie Leidig stood by his horse. The official party escorted him to Chris Jorgensen's studio, where they all remained for fifteen minutes. Roosevelt went in and looked at Jorgensen's paintings, and the artist served him a glass of champagne. The president thanked the Jorgensens for their courtesy in offering their home and apologized for not accepting.

Accompanied by five or six members of his party, Roosevelt walked back across the Sentinel Bridge to his horse. Muir had joined the president at the Jorgensen studio. The original party of five mounted their horses and started down the valley to pick a campsite near Bridalveil Fall, where Muir had suggested they spend the last night in camp. As they left the bridge, the president saw Ellen Boysen standing by her mother on the ground holding a flag. He reached down, picked her up under her arms, and kissing her said, "God bless you, you little angel." Putting her down, he waved his party off and started down the valley. They went down the south side of the river followed by a big string of people on horseback, in buggies, in surries, and on foot. Leidig estimated that there must have been 300 or 500, or possibly 1,000 of them in the crowd, filling the Bridalveil Meadows.

As they reached their camping places on a grassy slope just south of the present road through the meadow, the president said to Leidig, "These people annoy me. Can you get rid of them?" Leidig walked out and told the crowd that Roosevelt was very tired and asked them to leave. They went—some of them even on tiptoe, so as not to annoy their president. When Leidig returned to the campsite, the president said, "Charlie, I am hungry as hell. Cook any damn thing you wish. How long will it take?" Leidig told him it would take about thirty minutes, so Roosevelt lay on his bed of blankets, went to sleep, and snored so loudly that Leidig could hear him even above the crackling of the campfire. People came again in the morning. Crowds could be seen all through the brush. Leidig kept them away. The stage came down containing the president's official party. After breakfast, Roosevelt and Muir got into the stage, and as they left the president called Leidig and Leonard to him and said, "Boys, I am leaving you. Good-bye, and God bless you."

The individual accounts of the trip are fascinating, each one providing its own detail and perspective. The *San Francisco Call* did an excellent job covering the journey as evidenced by this story, which ran on May 18:

President Roosevelt arrived here at 10:30 o'clock this morning in excellent spirits. He was driven by Thomas Gordon, the famous stage driver, who has handled the ribbons on the Yosemite stage and turnpike companies line for the last 30 years. The president's party picked him up at Bridal Veil Meadows at 7 AM. Several in the president's party said they had never seen Mr. Roosevelt so buoyant before. He was thoroughly rested and said he had never felt better in his life. The crisp mountain air seems to have given him a new lease on life. He spoke rapturously all the way out to no one on the wonders of the Sierras, saying he had no idea of the sublime scenery and the magnitude of the forests before, and that no tale of the West, how marvelous it might be, could now astonish him.

The president also remarked on the amazing appetite he had and how good everything tasted in the woods. He suggested that Charles Lake, his cook and guide, should be a famous restaurateur. The Washburn brothers had furnished Leidig with the best kind of steaks and young broilers. These were lighting cooked over the coals and they appealed strongly to the president.

The nation's chief also commented upon the horses in the mountains. Never did he think a horse could take them down such steep trails, jump such logs, wade through such snow and, with it all, keep up such high spirits as the horse Para did. One place was so steep that he went over his head into the snow. He complemented Ms. Alice Bruce highly upon the virtues of her horse and said Para was the means of giving him three of the most delightful days of his life. In thanking you in Washburn for his courtesies he said his trip had been one of perfection.

An elaborate luncheon was served to the party here. A very pretty incident happened after lunch. Thomas Hill, the famous landscape artist of the Yosemite, was presented to the president. Mr. Roosevelt seemed much pleased, saying he had heard of Mr. Hill for many years and considered it a great honor to meet such a talented man. He then asked to be taken to his studio. The president greatly admired a large painting of the Bridalveil Fall with the meadows in the foreground, where he had spent the night. Mr. Hill surprised him by presenting him with the painting. The president was delighted and said the picture would always be dear to him on account of the associations… [I discovered something about this painting that makes it quite special, to be discussed at the end of this book.] *At 12 o'clock sharp the four presidential coaches drove up to the door and the president departed amid the cheers of the people. The president and party arrived safely at Raymond at 6 PM and boarded their special train, all happy and pleased over the Sierras and the Yosemite. The run from Ahwanee to Raymond was the dustiest part of the trip and the president and his traveling companions were badly in need of baths when they reached the train. An escort of cavalry from Fort Ward, which is situated here, went with the president to Raymond.*

Writer Hank Johnston included this in his article in Yosemite *magazine about the camping trip's finale: On the morning of May 18, Muir and the presidents joined the other members of the official party for the cannonball stage to return to the waiting special train at Raymond. The trip was important in itself because driver Tom Gordon set a record for speed that was never equaled in the 40 years of horse-drawn vehicles. In just 10 hours of actual driving time the party covered the 67 miles from Yosemite Valley to Raymond. The total elapsed time was just short of 12 hours. When he arrived at Raymond, reporters asked him about the Yosemite adventure with Muir. The president told them he had thoroughly enjoyed it. "It was bully," he said. "I had the time of my life!"*

The May 18 edition of the *San Francisco Call*, filed from the town of Merced, included an interesting detail:

Pres. Roosevelt's train stopped here for a few minutes this evening and quite a number of people were at the station to greet the president. He responded with a short speech:

"Ladies and Gentlemen, I am glad to have the chance of stopping here to greet you, and to say how much I have enjoyed my trip up in your mountains and my whole trip through California. It has been the greatest possible pleasure to get out here. I have enjoyed seeing the mountains; I have enjoyed seeing your scenery; I have enjoyed witnessing the wonderful products of your climate and soil; but what I have enjoyed most has been the chance to see the men and women of California."

And John Muir, the naturalist, who accompanied the president through the Yosemite Valley, left the train here.

So with that, Muir and Roosevelt parted ways. "I stuffed him pretty well," Muir said later in a letter to Dr. C Hart Merriam about the trip, "regarding the timber thieves, the destructive work of the lumberman, and other spoilers of the forest."

That dialogue may have played a part in the president's subsequent pro-conservation actions. During the remainder of his term of office, Roosevelt assisted in adding 147 million acres to the country's forest reserves, created eighteen national monuments and used his influence in the establishment of five national parks by Congress.

For the next few days, Roosevelt reflected not just on Yosemite but on the entire state of California and how impressed he was by all of it. These were his words in the small town of Berenda:

My Friends and Fellow-Citizens: I am glad to have the chance of saying a word to you of this wonderful and fertile valley, the San Joaquin Valley (cheers and applause); and even glimpses I have got of it have made me appreciate its fertility. I am glad that the soil and the climate here are such as to give us that indispensable base of material prosperity, the foundation upon which we must rest, but, gentlemen and ladies, the thing that pleases me most, even more than the crops, is the men and women I meet. (Applause) I believe in your future, because I believe in you—not only in the climate and the soil. You can take the best climate and the best soil and put a poor, shiftless, trifling creature on the soil and you do not get any results. To take advantage of the greatest opportunities you must have the men. I fail to see how any public man cannot believe in the future of this country after he has gone, as I have gone, from one side of the continent to the other, from the Atlantic to the Pacific, and has met audiences everywhere to whom he can appeal in the name of the fundamental virtues of American citizenship, fundamental virtues that go to make up good men and good women everywhere, and have gone to make them up since time began. I believe not in brilliancy, not in genius, I believe in the ordinary, humdrum, work-a-day virtues that make a man a good man in his family, a good neighbor, a good man to deal with in business, a good man to deal with in the State, and when you have got a man with those characteristics in him you have a man who if the need comes will rise level to that need. There are any number of different kinds of work that we have to do, all of which have to be done. There is the work of the farmer, the work of the business man, the work of the skilled mechanic, the work of the men to whom I owe my safety every day and every night—the work of the railroad men; the work of the lawyer, the work of the sailor, the work of the soldier, the work in ten thousand ways; it is all good work; it does not make any difference what work the man is doing if he does it well. If the man is a slack, shiftless creature I wish we could get rid of him. He is of no use. In every occupation you will find some men whom you will have to carry. You cannot do much with them. Every one of us will stumble at times, and shame to the man who does not at such times stretch out a helping hand, but if the man lies down you cannot carry him to any permanent use. What I would plead for is that we recognize that fact, that we bring up our children to work, so that each respects the other. I do not care whether a man is a banker or a bricklayer; if he is a good banker or a good bricklayer he is a good citizen; if he is dishonest, if he is tricky, if he shirks his job or tries to cheat his neighbor, be he great or small, be he the poor man cheating the rich man, or the rich man oppressing the poor man, in either case he is a bad citizen. I thank you and want to say what a pleasure it has been to see you here this evening.

In Modesto he said:

I am very glad to catch this glimpse of you. I have passed four delightful days in your mountains up there in the Yosemite and I cannot say how much I have enjoyed them, but I have enjoyed even more my entire trip through California and the courtesy and hospitality with which I have been received. It has been a great pleasure to me to come from the East to the West, then west of the West to California, and to see your wonderful State. And while I have enjoyed it all, enjoyed seeing the soil and the climate, enjoyed witnessing the abounding prosperity that you have succeeded in making, the thing that I have enjoyed most has been seeing the men and women, the citizens of California, for that is what counts most in the long run. The soil and the climate will not count for anything if the people have not got it in them to take advantage of the soil and climate. I think I came to California a middling good American and I will go away a better American. It has been the greatest pleasure to see you all.

A day later, on May 19, Roosevelt sent this letter:

Sacramento, Cal.,

My dear Mr. Muir:

I enclose the three letters. I trust I need not tell you, my dear sir, how happy were the days in the Yosemite I owed to you, and how greatly I appreciated them. I shall never forget our three camps; the first in the solemn temple of the giant sequoias; the next in the snow storm among the silver firs near the brink of the cliff: and the third on the floor of the Yosemite, in the open valley fronting the stupendous rocky mass of El Capitan, with the falls thundering in the distance on either hand.

Good luck go with you always.

Faithfully yours,
Theodore Roosevelt

This was Roosevelt's speech in Sacramento that same day, as the trip pushed north:

Mr. Mayor, and you, My Fellow-Citizens, it is a great pleasure to have the chance of meeting you here in the capital city of your wonderful State. (Applause) In greeting all of you I know that the others will not grudge my saying a special word of acknowledgment to those whose mettle rang true on war's red touchstone, to the men to whom we owe it that we have tonight one country or that there is a President to speak to you—(applause)—the men of the Grand Army, the veterans of the great war, I wish also to express at this time my acknowledgments to my escort, the National Guard, many of them my comrades in the lesser war of '98. (Laughter and applause.) You see, in '98 we had a difficulty from which you were wholly free in '61, because with us there was not enough war to go around. (Applause)

I have enjoyed to the full my visit to California. I have come across the continent from the East to the West, and now beyond the West to California, for California stands by itself. (Applause) I have enjoyed every hour of my stay here. I have just come from a four days' rest in the Yosemite, and I wish to say one word to you here in the capital city of California about certain of your great natural resources, your forests and the water supply coming from the streams that find their sources among the forests of the mountains.

California possesses a wonderful climate, a wonderful soil, and throughout the portions that I have visited it is literally astounding to see how the land yields a hundred and a thousand fold when water is put upon it. And where it is possible to irrigate the land the result is, of course, far better than having to depend upon rainfall anywhere, but no small part of the prosperity of California in the hotter and drier agricultural regions depends upon the preservation of her water supply; and the water supply cannot be preserved unless the forests are preserved. (Applause) As regards some of the trees, I want them preserved because they are the only things of their kind in the world. Lying out at night under those giant Sequoias was lying in a temple built by no hand of man, a temple grander than any human architect could by any possibility build, and I hope for the preservation of the groves of giant trees simply because it would be a shame to our civilization to let them disappear. They are monuments in themselves, I ask for the preservation of the other forests on grounds of wise and far-sighted economic policy. I do not ask that lumbering be stopped at all. On the contrary, I ask that the forests be kept for use in lumbering, only that they be so used that not only shall we here, this generation, get the benefit for the next few years, but that our children and our children's children shall get the benefit. In California I am impressed by how great the State is, but I am even more impressed by the immensely greater greatness that lies in the future, and I ask that your marvelous natural resources be handed on unimpaired to your posterity. (Applause) We are not building this country of ours for a day. It is to last through the ages. We stand on the threshold of a new century. We look into the dim years that rise before us, knowing that if we are true that the generations that succeed us here shall fall heir to a heritage such as has never been known before. I ask that we keep in mind not only our own interests, but the interests of our children. Any generation fit to do its work must work for the future, for the people of the future, as well as for itself. You, men of the Civil War, fought from '61 to '65 for the Union of that day; yes, and for the Union that was to stand while nations stand in the hereafter. (Applause) You fought to make the flag that had been rent asunder once more whole and without a seam and to float over you and to float over all who come after you likewise. You fought for the future; you fought for the looming greatness of the republic in the centuries that were to come, and now I ask that we, in fulfilling the duties of citizenship, keep our gaze fixed likewise on the days that are to come after us. You are building here this great State within whose bounds lies an area as great as an Old World empire, a State with a commerce already vast, but with a commerce which within the century that has now opened shall cover and dominate the entire Pacific Ocean. (Applause) You are building your factories, you are tilling the fields; business man, professional man, farmer, wage-worker, all here in this State see a future of unknown possibilities opening before them.

I earnestly ask that you see to it that your resources, by use, are perpetuated for the use of the peoples yet unborn. Use them, but in using, keep and preserve them. Keep the waters; keep the forests; use your lands as you use your bays, your harbors, as you use the cities here, so that by the very fact of the use they will become more valuable as possessions.

I have spoken of the material things, of the things which are indispensable as the foundation, the base of national greatness. We must care for the body first. We must see to it that our tremendous industrial development goes on, that the well-being continues; that the soil yields its wealth in the future as it has in the past, aye, and tenfold more. We cannot for one moment afford to underestimate the vital importance of that material well-being, of the prosperity which we so abundantly enjoy, but I ask also that you remember the things of the mind and the soul as well as the body. Nothing has struck me more in going through California than the interest you are paying to the cause of education, than the way in which your citizens evidently realize that upon the proper training of the children, of those who are to be the men and women of a score of years hence, depends the ultimate welfare of the republic. Let me draw a lesson from you, the men of the Civil War. You needed strong bodies, you needed the supplies, the arms, but more than all, you needed the hearts that drove the bodies into battle. What distinguished our men was the spirit that drove them onward to effort and to strife, onward into action, onward through the march, through the long months of waiting in camp, onward through the fiery ordeal of battle, when men's souls were winnowed out as before the judgment seat. You then rose level to the duty that was before you because of the spirit that burned within your breasts, because you had in you the capacity of generous enthusiasm for the lofty ideal, because you realized that there was something above the body and greater than the body. And now, my fellows, men and women of California, men and women of the American Union, I ask throughout this country that our people keep in their hearts the capacity of devotion to what stands above mere bodily welfare, to the welfare of the spirit, of the mind, of the soul. I ask that we have strong bodies, well cared for, well clothed, well housed. I ask for what is better than a strong body, a sane mind. And I ask finally for what counts for more than body, for more than mind, for character; character which in the last analysis tells most in settling the welfare of either a nation or an individual; character into which many elements enter, but three, above all; in the first place, as a foundation, decency, honesty, morality, the quality that makes a man a good husband, a good neighbor, a man who deals fairly and squarely with those about him, who does his duty to those around him and to the State; and that is not enough. Decency and honesty are not enough. Just as in the Civil War you needed patriotism first, but it made no matter how patriotic a man was, if he ran away you could do nothing with him. (Applause) So in civic life you must have decency and honesty, for without them ability makes a man only the more dangerous to his fellows, the greater force for evil. Just again as in the Civil War, if the man did not have in him the capacity of loyalty to his fellows, loyalty to his regiment, loyalty to the flag, if he did not have in him that capacity, the abler he was the worse he was to have in the army. So it is now in civil life; the abler a man is, if he has not the root of righteousness in him the more dangerous a foe to decent government he is, and we shall never rise level to the needs of our nation until we make it understood that the scoundrel who succeeds is to be hunted down by public opinion, by the condemnation and scorn of his fellows, exactly as we hunt down the weaker scoundrel who fails.

(Applause) But that is not enough. Decency and honesty are a basis, but that is all. I do not care how moral a man is, if his morality is only good while he sits at home in his own parlor, you can do nothing with him. Scant is the use we have for the timid good. In the war you needed patriotism, and then you needed the fighting edge. You had to have that. So in civil life we need the spirit of decency, of honesty, and then, in addition, the quality of courage, of hardihood, of manliness, that makes a man fit to go out into the hurly-burly and do a man's work in the world. That must come, too; and that is not enough. I do not care how moral a man is and how brave he is, if he is a natural born fool you can do nothing with him. I ask, then, for decency as the foundation, for courage and manliness thereon, and finally, in addition to both, I ask for common sense as the moderator and guide of both. (Applause)

My fellow-countrymen, I believe in you; I believe in your future; I believe in the future of the American republic, because I believe that the average American citizen has in him just those qualities—the quality of honesty, the quality of courage, and the quality of common sense. While we keep in the community the power of adherence to a lofty ideal and at the same time the power to attempt its realization by practical methods, we can be sure that our progress in the future will be even more rapid than our progress has been in the past, and that in the century now opening, in the centuries that succeed it, this country, already the greatest republic upon which the sun has ever shone, will attain a position of prominence in the world's history that will dwarf into insignificance all that has ever been done before.

May 20 would be the president's last day in California, and his poetic enthusiasm for the state continued with speeches in several cities and towns approaching the state's northern border:

May 20, Redding

My Friends and Fellow-Citizens: It is a great pleasure to see you today. This is to be my last day in California, and I leave the State with the liveliest appreciation of the courtesy with which I have been received, and with memories which I shall ever keep of the pleasant days I have had within your borders. I have seen pretty much all the State from the ocean up to the Sierras and into them; I have come from the south and am leaving at the northern end; and I am impressed, as every man must be, with what our nation is to have within its borders a State such as this, a State in resources and size the equal to many an Old World empire. (Applause) I have enjoyed everything, seeing your farms, your ranches, your cities, noting the diversification of your industries, seeing the products of the ranch, of the irrigated agriculture, of the mine, of the forest, realizing as a man must, who sees San Francisco and that wonderful harbor that here is one of the cities which must in time now near do its full share in dominating the commerce of the world. (Applause) I have enjoyed all of these sights; but most of all I have enjoyed seeing you, the men and women of California. (Applause) That is what counts ultimately in any nation. We need of course the physical advantages, but they are useless if we have not got the men to take advantage of them. Constitution, laws—they are good things, indispensable things, to have right, but you must have the men behind them or they will amount to but little. There are other nations with the same type of constitution, the same theoretical form of government as ours, and yet those other nations have failed where we have succeeded because the type of citizenship was different. So here, the climate and soil would amount to nothing, if you did not have men and women of the right type to take advantage of them.

You here in California, who succeeded the pioneers, you have won your place by showing the qualities which we like to think of as typical of American citizens. If we of this great Republic are to continue in the future to rise level to our opportunities as our forefathers rose in the past, we must so rise by showing the traits, which they showed. There is no patent recipe for making a good citizen any more than there is any patent recipe for making a successful man. Success will come in the long run to the man or the nation possessing the attributes that have conquered success from the days when we first have written records of the nations of mankind. If our people have courage, perseverance, self-restraint, self-mastery, will power and common sense—you need that always—we will win out. I said common sense; I think that there is only one quality worse than hardness of heart and that is softness of head. I want to see the average American citizen be in the future as he has been in the past, a decent man, doing no wrong, and on the other hand able to hold his own also; and just as I want to see with the average citizen, I want to see with the nation.

In Dunsmuir, the president said:

It is a great pleasure to greet you today. I have enjoyed the last two hours traveling up by this beautiful river and getting my first glimpses of Shasta.

It has been a very great pleasure to come here to this State beside the Pacific Ocean and see your people. I think I can say that I came to California a pretty good American, and I go away a better one. (Applause) Glad though I have been to see your wonderful products, your plains and your mountains, your rivers, to see the great cities springing up, most of all have I enjoyed meeting the men and women to whom we owe what has been done with mine and railroad and lumbering camp and irrigated field, with the ranch and the counting-house—the men and women who have made California what she is.

Almost everywhere I have been greeted by men who are veterans of the Civil War; or else by men who came here in the early pioneer days; and where that has not been the case I have met those who are their worthy successors, who are doing now the kind of work that is worth doing. I pity no man because he has to work. If he is worth his salt he will work. I envy the man who has a work worth doing and does it well; and surely no men alive are more worthy of admiration than those men to whom it is given to build up a giant commonwealth like this. It is the fact of doing the work well that counts, not the kind of work, as long as that work is honorable.

I speak to citizens of a community which has reached its present pitch of prosperity because they have done each his duty as his lines were laid. To the true American nothing can be more alien than the spirit either of envy or of contempt for another who is leading a life as a decent citizen should lead it. In this country we have room for every honest man who spends his life in honest effort; we have no room either for the man of means who, in a spirit of arrogant baseness, looks down upon the man less well off, or for the other man who envies his neighbor because that neighbor happens to be better off. Either feeling is a base feeling, unworthy of a self-respecting man.

I used the word envy, myself, just now, but I did not use it in a bad sense. If you use envy in the ordinary sense of the word its existence implies a feeling of inferiority in the man who feels it, a feeling that a self-respecting man will be ashamed to have. If the man is a good American and is doing his work squarely he need not envy anybody, because he occupies a position such as no one else in any other country, in any other age has occupied; and because we hold our citizenship so high, because we feel and have the right to feel satisfaction with what our people have done, we should also feel that the only spirit in which to regard any other man who does well, is a spirit of kindly regard and good will if he acts squarely; if he does not, then I think but ill of you if you do not regard him as a man to feel at least the public scorn, public contempt. It is, of course, a perfectly trite saying that

Roosevelt speaking in the logging town of Dunsmuir, California, on May 20.

in no country is it so necessary to have decency, honesty, self-restraint, in the average citizen as in a republic, in a democracy; for successful self-government is founded upon that high average of citizenship among our people; and America has gone on as she has gone because we have had that high average of citizenship. Our government is based upon the rule of a self-respecting majority. Our government has so far escaped the twin dangers of the older republics, government by a plutocracy or government by a mob, either of them absolutely alien to American ideals.

It has been a great pleasure to see you. I haven't any special word of preaching to say, because after all, men and women of California, I can only preach what in substance you have practiced, what our people have

Roosevelt gives a speech in Eureka, California.

practiced in the making and carrying on of this government. From the days of Washington to the days of Lincoln we went onward and upward because the average American was of the stuff that made the nation go onward and upward. We cannot be dragged up, we have got to push ourselves up. No law that ever was devised can give wisdom to the fool, courage to the coward, strength to the weakling. We must have those qualities in us, for if they are not in us they cannot be gotten out of us. Of course all you have to do is to compare what other nations have done with governments founded as ours, the same type of constitution, the same type of law, which nevertheless have failed, have produced chaos because they did not have the right type of citizen back of the law, the right type of citizen to work out the destiny of the Nation under and through the law. Of course we need the right law; we need even more the honest and fearless enforcement of the law, enforcement in a spirit of absolute fair play to all men, showing favoritism to none, doing justice to each. We need such laws, such administration of the laws, but most of all we need to keep up that for the lack of which nothing else can atone in any people—the average standard of citizenship—so that the average man shall have certain fundamental qualities that come under many different heads, but under three especially. In the first place, that he shall have at the foundation of his character the moral forces, the forces that make a man a good husband, a good father, a good neighbor, a man who deals fairly by his fellows, whether he works with them on the railroad or in the shops or in the factories, whether he deals with them as a mechanic, as a lawyer, as a doctor, whether he grows the products of the soil as an earth-tiller, a miner, a lumberman, a sailor, whatever he is, whatever his wealth, if he acts squarely he has fulfilled the first requisites of citizenship. We cannot afford in our Republic to draw distinctions between our citizens save on that line of conduct. There are good men and bad men everywhere. All of you know them in private life; all of you have met them. You have got to have decency and morality in the first place, and, of course, that is not enough. It does not begin to be enough. No matter how decent a man is, if he is afraid he is no good. In addition to the quality of self-mastery, self-restraint, decency, you have got to have the quality of hardihood, courage, manliness, the quality which, if the people who founded this State had lacked, there never would have been a State founded here. You have got to have the men who can hold their own in work, and, if necessary, in fighting. You have got to have those qualities in addition, and you have got to have others still. I do not care how brave a man is and how decent he is, if he is a natural born fool you can do very little with him. In addition to decency, in addition to courage, you must have the saving grace of common sense; the quality that enables any man to tell what he can do for himself and what he can do for his neighbor, for the nation. Sometimes each of us has the feeling that if he has to choose between the fool and the knave he will take the knave, because he can reform him perhaps, and he cannot reform the "fool"; and even hardness of heart is not much more destructive in the long run than softness of head.

In our life what we need is not so much genius, not so much brilliancy, as the ordinary commonplace everyday qualities which a man needs in private life, and which he needs just as much in public life.

In coming across the continent from the Atlantic to the Pacific, the thing that has struck me most is that, fundamentally, wherever one goes in this broad country, a good American is a good American. (Applause)

I thank you with all my heart for coming here, and I wish you all good fortune in the future as in the past.

These were the president's words in Montague:

It is a great pleasure to meet you this afternoon. I have enjoyed to the full my trip through California. I have come from the south through the State and now go out at the north. When the trip was made up I asked why it was necessary to give relatively four times as much time to California as to any other State. I understand now. (Applause) I only wish it had been possible to make it eight times as much instead. This morning I have been greatly impressed in traveling through these mountains and meeting the men who have done so much in lumbering, as I have already met the men of the mines, and ranches, of the commerce and industries of the great cities. This State is in boundaries and resources greater than many an Old World empire; and think what it is to be a citizen of a Union in which a commonwealth like this is a State. I have come from the Atlantic to the Pacific, from the East through the West to beyond the west to California, for that stands by itself. (Applause) The thing that has impressed me more than anything else in addressing the different audiences is that a good American is a good American in whatever part of this country he lives.

And finally, in the tiny speck called Hornbrook (which as of this writing boasts a population of just 248), Roosevelt made his last speech in California as part of the 1903 tour:

I have just said good-bye to the Governor of California, and I am very, very sorry to part with him. He has been with me throughout my trip in California, and I have gone pretty fairly over the State with him. Today I have been traveling through the northern part of California, among the mountains and the forests, and it has given me an ever fresh view of your wonderful and beautiful State. As I have said more than once since entering your State, I knew as no one knows by reading and by hearing people talk of all the resources that it had, but I could not fully realize them until I had seen them. Going through California, I have been struck with the prosperous and contented look of its people, and of course you are contented; I should be ashamed of you if you were not (applause), living in such a State as this. And glad though I have been to see your soil and climate, to see your products, the products of your fields, and mines and woods, what you have done with railroads, with transportation companies on the water, with factories, with industries of every kind, what I have been most pleased with after all has been the way in which you are training the citizenship of the future, the attention paid to the schools of every grade here in this State; and above all with the type of men and women and children whom it has been my good fortune to encounter. The essential thing in any State is the character of the average man or woman, and I am proud to be your fellow-citizen, and to have men the type of people I have met in California.

Chapter 6
HEADING BACK HOME

Later on Wednesday, May 20, Roosevelt's the train crossed into Oregon, and the California portion of the journey was over. In Portland on May 21, Roosevelt laid a cornerstone for the Lewis and Clark monument. Then it was on to Olympia and Tacoma in the state of Washington, before reaching Seattle the next day, where Roosevelt took a trip on Puget Sound to inspect the Bremerton Navy Yard. Continuing east, there were speeches at Cle Elum, Ellensburg, North Yakima, Pasco and Walla Walla, Washington, among several other stops. The next day, he spoke at Spokane, and then it was on to Idaho.

On Wednesday the twenty-seventh, the president arrived in Montana, and his visit to Butte was described in a letter that Roosevelt wrote to John Hay in August 1903: "In Butte every prominent man is a millionaire, a professional gambler, or labor leaders; and generally he has been all three. Of the hundred men who were my hosts I suppose at least half had killed their man in private war, or had striven to compass the assassination of an enemy. They had fought one another with reckless ferocity. They had been allies and enemies in every kind of business scheme, and companions and brutal revelry. As they drank great goblets of wine this sweat glistened on their hard, strong, crafty faces."

In Boise, Idaho, on May 28, the president commented, "I was struck by the growing beauty of the town, by the trees, the well-built public library, the good taste and refinement evident in the dress, the bearing, and the homes of the people."

Left: Roosevelt on deck enjoying a friendly chat and the invigorating air of Puget Sound along the coast of Washington State.

Below: Indians racing with the president's train under snow-streaked Idaho mountains near Pocatello, Idaho.

The next few days found the president speaking throughout Utah and Wyoming, where on June 1, he went to the Wild West Exhibition at Frontier Park. He was presented with a complete riding outfit—a gift of the people of Cheyenne and Douglas, who were represented by Senator Francis Warren. While at Cheyenne, Roosevelt heard of the destructive flooding that was happening at Topeka and sent the following telegram to the people of Kansas: "Inexpressibly shocked at reports of dreadful calamity that has befallen to pick up. If there is anything the federal authorities can do, of course let me know."

President Roosevelt and a responsive audience at Ogden, Utah.

At Sidney, Nebraska, the president made an address on good citizenship to a large crowd. He stopped at North Platte and then gave brief speeches at Lexington and Kearney. On June 2, the train entered Iowa and was turned over by the Union Pacific to the Illinois Central. It passed through the flooded districts of Iowa, but precautions had been taken to ensure the safety of the train tracks.

Brief stops were made at Webster City, Iowa Falls, Cedar Falls, Waterloo, Manchester and Independence, with the president speaking a few words from his train platform to people who were eagerly awaiting his arrival. The day's journey ended at Dubuque, where Roosevelt was received with a cannon salute and the cheers of thousands as he stepped from the train. At least twenty thousand people lined the streets over which his carriage was driven. At the city park, he gave a brief speech to six thousand schoolchildren, who sang "America" to him. After a tour of the hills overlooking the Mississippi River, Roosevelt spoke to one thousand people at the Dubuque Club. The trip was nearing its close.

At Freeport, Illinois, the morning of June 3, the president was driven to the site of the Lincoln-Douglas debate in 1858, where a monument commemorating the event was unveiled in the presence of many thousands of people from the area. Later, he spoke to fifteen thousand people at Lincoln Park and Pontiac, where the president took part in the dedication of a soldiers and sailors monument. The night was spent in Bloomington, Illinois, and the next day it was on to Springfield, where twenty thousand visitors greeted the president at the station. In a speech to veterans here, Roosevelt said, "It was my good fortune at Santiago to serve beside colored troops. A man who is good enough to shed his blood for the country is good enough to be given a square deal afterward. More than that no man is entitled to, and less than that no man shall have." Roosevelt also visited the tomb of Abraham Lincoln.

After stops in Decatur and Danville, the president reached Indianapolis at 9:05 p.m., where five thousand people met him at the station. "I have been from the Atlantic to the Pacific and now well nigh back to the Atlantic again, he told them, and the thing that has struck me more than anything else wherever I have been is the fundamental mental unity of our people."

On June 5, the train stopped at Pittsburgh at 8:22 a.m., and the president stepped out onto the rear platform to tell the waiting masses, "I am happy to be with you; happy to get back from my trip. Good luck to you all." At Altoona, there was an immense crowd, and the president wished those in attendance good luck and bid them farewell. The train passed through Harrisburg and

Security forces on horseback guard Roosevelt's train.

Baltimore, and the trip officially came to an end in Washington, D.C., at 7:00 p.m. on June 5, 1903. As the papers reported:

> *President Roosevelt returned to Washington at 7 o'clock tonight from his memorable trip of over two months throughout the West. He was given a hearty reception by the people of the Capitol lining the sidewalks as his carriage, escorted by the battalion of high school cadets, was driven to the White House. The president cordially responded to the greetings given him and repeatedly stood up in his carriage and waved his hand and bowed his acknowledgments. He looked the picture of health.*

The trip just completed has been in some respects the most remarkable ever taken. Mr. Roosevelt's party traveled over 14,000 miles on railroads and several hundred miles in stagecoaches and carriages, but not an accident marred the journey. Not five minutes delay was occasioned during the whole trip on account of train conditions and the schedule adopted by Secretary Loeb before the party left Washington was carried out with military precision. Rarely was the train late in reaching its destination, notwithstanding it passed through the flooded district of Iowa. The health of the president and his party, too, was remarkably good. Not one member of the party was seriously ill and few calls were made on the physician. During the 65 days the president spent on the road he made 265 speeches and had it not been for Secretary's Loeb's firmness he would have made nearly double that number. From the day the president left Washington, requests began to pour in for changes in his program and for additional addresses, but Sec. Loeb in almost every case said no. The manner in which Mr. Loeb managed the trip was very pleasing to the president and he warmly congratulated his secretary on the successful outcome of it. The other members of the party also gave Mr. Loeb vote of thanks for the able manner in which he had conducted affairs.

One of the remarkable features of the trip was the nonpartisan feeling displayed in the reception of the president everywhere. Democratic as well as Republican mayors united in extending him a welcoming hand and while at Springfield, Illinois, former VP Stephenson rode in the carriage with the president. The crowds were orderly and friendly and gave the Secret Service men little cause for concern. These men were under the command of Frank Tyree who is detailed at the White House and the able manner in which they performed their task was the subject of general commendation.

Chapter 7

THE LASTING EFFECTS
OF THE CAMPING TRIP

Earlier in this book, I included the first part of a 1955 article entitled "Roosevelt and Muir—Conservationists," written by ranger-naturalist Richard J. Hartesveldt. Here is the rest of the wonderful piece he penned, which details a large part of Theodore Roosevelt's conservationist legacy:

"THE POWER TO PROTECT"

Now, with the power to proclaim lands as monuments in the public interest, Roosevelt in 1908 set aside some 800,000 acres as Grand Canyon National Monument. Congress later gave it a national park status.

Park areas set aside during the Roosevelt era included: Chaco Canyon, New Mexico; Devils Tower, Wyoming; El Morro, New Mexico; Gila Cliff Dwellings, New Mexico; Jewel Cave, South Dakota; Montezuma Castle, Arizona; Muir Woods, California; Natural Bridges, Utah; Navajo, Arizona; Pinnacles, California; Tonto, Arizona; Petrified Forest, Arizona; Tumacacori, Arizona, and Lassen Peak and Cinder Cone, California (now Lassen Volcanic National Park).

Conservation of our natural resources became a major part of Roosevelt's activities. The monopolistic misuses of lands acquired from public domain largely came to an end.

Land users, some with great resentment, were required to pay for the privilege of that use. Even the enemies of this historic change had to admit its benefit to the country at large. The tide had turned.

In May 1908, the President called the Conference of Governors at the White House. Governors of every state and territory, the Cabinet, the Supreme Court justices and numerous senators and representatives were invited to discuss what TR considered to be the greatest problem confronting the nation.

He must have thought it of utmost importance to have called the governors away from their jobs all at once. The conference was unique and the President gained world-wide prestige because of it.

LOOKING AHEAD

Here, in a time of plenty, he was calling the nation to look ahead and plan wisely for the continuous use of the rich resources. As a result of this conference nearly every state established a conservation commission.

From this evolved the National Conservation Commission which carried on its activities mainly on TR spirit, since there was little or no money for its operation.

In 1909, Roosevelt initiated the North American Conservation Conference, inviting Canada, Newfoundland and Mexico to participate in a discussion of common resource problems.

A worldwide conference was proposed and was to be held at the Hague, Netherlands. However, it never materialized because of a lesser interest in conservation on the part of his successor, William Howard Taft.

Among his other great accomplishments was the formulation of the Inland Waterways Commission which was instrumental in showing the close relationship between forests and water flow.

Waterway development became a scientific and intelligent business for the first time. Mineral and oil lands were saved from exploitation.

The Division of Forestry under Gifford Pinchot was greatly strengthened and 148 million acres of forest land was given national forest status. During the Roosevelt administration 234 million acres of land were withdrawn from private entry, to be managed for the benefit of the American people.

A MEANINGFUL LEGACY

The amount that John Muir influenced Teddy Roosevelt's subsequent courageous actions in behalf of the public is as intangible as is the value of Yosemite's famous scenery. Few will deny that the value was great. The people of the United States will long reap the benefits of a program which was strongly encouraged around their campfires in Yosemite National Park.

In 1903, President Theodore Roosevelt visited Yosemite and spent four days camping with John Muir. Their conversations focused on the protection of our national treasures. During this visit, Roosevelt met Thomas Hill at his studio. Hill gave Roosevelt a painting of Bridalveil Fall that he had admired, and it returned with him to the White House. Today—in writing, photography, painting, music, American Indian art and other media—our national parks continue to inspire artists from around the world. The magnificent scenic and cultural legacy of these places and the stories they tell are a testament to the legacy of park preservation and are an inspiration to each generation.

Theodore Roosevelt and John Muir stayed in touch for the next eleven years until Muir passed away. Many letters attest to their friendships and concerns for each other. In April 1908, Muir raised an issue with Roosevelt—something that would become his last crusade. He wanted to prevent the City of San Francisco from building a dam and creating a massive water reservoir in Yosemite's Hetch Hetchy Valley. In part, the letter read:

> *I am anxious that the Yosemite National Park may be saved from all sorts of commercialism and marks of man's work other than the roads, hotels etc required to make its wonders and blessings available. For as far as I have seen there is not in all the wonderful Sierra, or indeed in the world another so grand and wonderful and useful a block of Nature's mountain handiwork. There is now under consideration, as doubtless you well know, an application of San Francisco Supervisors for the use of Hetch Hetchy Valley and Lake Eleanor as storage reservoirs for a City water supply. This application should I think be denied especially the Hetch Hetchy part, for this Valley as you will see by the enclosed description is a counterpart of Yosemite, and one of the most sublime and beautiful and important features of the Park, and to dam and submerge it would be hardly less destructive and deplorable in its effects on the Park in general than would be the damming of Yosemite itself. For its falls and groves and delightful camp-grounds are surpassed or equaled only in Yosemite: and furthermore it is the hall of entrance to the grand Tuolumne Canyon which opens a wonderful way to the magnificent Tuolumne Meadows, the focus of pleasure travel in the High Sierra of the Park and grand central camp-ground. If Hetch Hetchy should be submerged as proposed to a depth of 175 feet, not only would it be made utterly inaccessible, but this glorious canyon way to the High Sierra would be blocked.*

Muir and Roosevelt would meet once more, at a stag dinner held for the former president in Pasadena in 1911, and Muir pled his case even further. But Roosevelt was no longer in a position to help as he had been years before. The battle went on for years, despite Muir rallying as many groups as he could; the fight for Hetch Hetchy ended in bitter defeat with federal approval of the project in 1913. When Woodrow Wilson signed into law the bill allowing a dam in Hetch Hetchy, Muir wrote to a friend, "It is a monumental mistake, but it is more, it is a monumental crime." In poor health, Muir died the next year on December 24, 1914.

In January 1915, Roosevelt wrote this piece in honor of his friend and onetime camping buddy:

John Muir: An Appreciation
by Theodore Roosevelt

Our greatest nature lover and nature writer, the man who has done most in securing for the American people the incalculable benefit of appreciation of wild nature in his own land, is John Burroughs. Second only to John Burroughs, and in some respects ahead even of John Burroughs, was John Muir. Ordinarily, the man who loves the woods and mountains, the trees, the flowers, and the wild things, has in him some indefinable quality of charm, which appeals even to those sons of civilization who care for little outside of paved streets and brick walls. John Muir was a fine illustration of this rule. He was by birth a Scotchman—a tall and spare man, with the poise and ease natural to him who has lived much alone under conditions of labor and hazard. He was a dauntless soul, and also one brimming over with friendliness and kindliness.

He was emphatically a good citizen. Not only are his books delightful, not only is he the author to whom all men turn when they think of the Sierras and northern glaciers, and the giant trees of the California slope, but he was also—what few nature lovers are—a man able to influence contemporary thought and action on the subjects to which he had devoted his life. He was a great factor in influencing the thought of California and the thought of the entire country so as to secure the preservation of those great natural phenomena—wonderful canyons, giant trees, slopes of flower-spangled hillsides—which make California a veritable Garden of the Lord.

It was my good fortune to know John Muir. He had written me, even before I met him personally, expressing his regret that when Emerson came to see the Yosemite, his [Emerson's] friends would not allow him to accept

John Muir's invitation to spend two or three days camping with him, so as to see the giant grandeur of the place under surroundings more congenial than those of a hotel piazza or a seat on a coach. I had answered him that if ever I got in his neighborhood I should claim from him the treatment that he had wished to accord Emerson. Later, when as President I visited the Yosemite, John Muir fulfilled the promise he had at that time made to me. He met me with a couple of pack mules, as well as with riding mules for himself and myself, and a first-class packer and cook, and I spent a delightful three days and two nights with him.

The first night we camped in a grove of giant sequoias. It was clear weather, and we lay in the open, the enormous cinnamon-colored trunks rising about us like the columns of a vaster and more beautiful cathedral than was ever conceived by any human architect. One incident surprised me not a little. Some thrushes—I think they were Western hermit-thrushes—were singing beautifully in the solemn evening stillness. I asked some question concerning them of John Muir, and to my surprise found that he had not been listening to them and knew nothing about them. Once or twice I had been off with John Burroughs, and had found that, although he was so much older than I was, his ear and his eye were infinitely better as regards the sights and sounds of wild life, or at least of the smaller wild life, and I was accustomed unhesitatingly to refer to him regarding any bird note that puzzled me. But John Muir, I found, was not interested in the small things of nature unless they were unusually conspicuous. Mountains, cliffs, trees, appealed to him tremendously, but birds did not unless they possessed some very peculiar and interesting as well as conspicuous traits, as in the case of the water ouzel. In the same way, he knew nothing of the wood mice; but the more conspicuous beasts, such as bear and deer, for example, he could tell much about.

All next day we traveled through the forest. Then a snow-storm came on, and at night we camped on the edge of the Yosemite, under the branches of a magnificent silver fir, and very warm and comfortable we were, and a very good dinner we had before we rolled up in our tarpaulins and blankets for the night. The following day we went down into the Yosemite and through the valley, camping in the bottom among the timber.

There was a delightful innocence and good will about the man, and an utter inability to imagine that any one could either take or give offense. Of this I had an amusing illustration just before we parted. We were saying good-by, when his expression suddenly changed, and he remarked that he had totally forgotten something. He was intending to go to the Old World *with a great tree lover and tree expert from the Eastern States who possessed a somewhat crotchety temper. He informed me that his friend had written him, asking him to get from me personal letters to the Russian Czar and the Chinese Emperor; and when I explained to him that I could not give personal letters to foreign potentates, he said: "Oh, well, read the letter yourself, and that will explain just what I want." Accordingly, he thrust the letter on me. It contained not only the request which he had mentioned, but also a delicious preface, which, with the request, ran somewhat as follows:*

"I hear Roosevelt is coming out to see you. He takes a sloppy, unintelligent interest in forests, although he is altogether too much under the influence of that creature Pinchot, and you had better get from him letters to the Czar of Russia and the Emperor of China, so that we may have better opportunity to examine the forests and trees of the Old World."

Of course I laughed heartily as I read the letter, and said, "John, do you remember exactly the words in which this letter was couched?" Whereupon a look of startled surprise came over his face, and he said: "Good gracious! There was something unpleasant about you in it; wasn't there? I had forgotten. Give me the letter back."

So I gave him back the letter, telling him that I appreciated it far more than if it had not contained the phrases he had forgotten, and that while I could not give him and his companion letters to the two rulers in question, I would give him letters to our Ambassadors, which would bring about the same result.

John Muir talked even better than he wrote. His greatest influence was always upon those who were brought into personal contact with him. But he wrote well, and while his books have not the peculiar charm that a very, very few other writers on similar subjects have had, they will nevertheless last long. Our generation owes much to John Muir.

Of course, we also owe much to Roosevelt. As the National Park Service noted in an online article:

Some of Theodore Roosevelt's greatest accomplishments were in conservation. In 1905, President Roosevelt formed the United States Forestry Service and appointed Gifford Pinchot as the first chief of this new agency. Under TR's direction, lands were reserved for public use and huge irrigation projects were started. During Roosevelt's time as President, the forest reserves in the U.S. went from approximately 43-million acres to about 194-million acres.

As President, he signed legislation that established five national park units: Crater Lake, Oregon; Wind Cave, South Dakota; Sullys Hill, North Dakota (later designated a game preserve); Mesa Verde, Colorado; and Platt, Oklahoma (now part of the Chickasaw National Recreation Area). By the end of 1906, Roosevelt had proclaimed four national monuments: Devil's Tower, Wyoming; El Morro, New Mexico; Montezuma Castle, Arizona; and the Petrified Forest, Arizona. He also protected a large portion of the Grand Canyon as a national monument in 1908. During his presidency, TR signed into law a total of 18 national monuments.

The Antiquities Act of June 8, 1906 had an even broader effect. Although the Act did not create a single park, it allowed Roosevelt and his successors to proclaim "historic landmarks, historic or prehistoric structures, and other objects of historic or scientific interest" in federal ownership as national monuments. Roosevelt's actions in conservation helped to impact what would one day become the National Park Service (NPS), which was formally established on August 25, 1916.

In his own words, Theodore Roosevelt strongly believed in conserving our national lands.

"I recognize the right and duty of this generation to develop and use the nature resources of our land; but I do not recognize the right to waste them, or to rob, by wasteful use, the generations that come after us." (Theodore Roosevelt, Osawatomie, Kansas, August 31, 1910).

NATIONAL PARKS AND MONUMENTS ESTABLISHED BY THEODORE ROOSEVELT

- Crater Lake National Park (Oregon), 1902
- Wind Cave National Park (South Dakota), 1903
- Sullys Hill (North Dakota), 1904 (now managed by U.S. Fish and Wildlife Service)
- Platt National Park (Oklahoma), 1906 (now part of Chickasaw National Recreation Area)
- Mesa Verde National Park (Colorado), 1906
- land added to Yosemite National Park

National Monuments

Roosevelt signed the Act for the Preservation of American Antiquities, also know as the Antiquities Act or the National Monuments Act, on June 8, 1906. The law authorized the president, at his discretion, to "declare by public proclamation historic landmarks, historic and prehistoric structures, and other objects of historic and scientific interest that are situated upon lands owned or controlled by the Government of the United States to be National Monuments."

- Devil's Tower, 1906
- El Morro, 1906
- Montezuma Castle, 1906
- Petrified Forest, 1906 (now a national park)
- Chaco Canyon, 1907
- Lassen Peak, 1907 (now a national park)
- Cinder Cone, 1907 (now part of Lassen Volcanic National Park)
- Gila Cliff Dwellings, 1907
- Tonto, 1907
- Muir Woods, 1908
- Grand Canyon, 1908 (now a national park; Roosevelt fought unsuccessfully to make it a national park in his time)
- Pinnacles, 1908?
- Jewel Cave, 1908?
- Natural Bridges, 1908
- Lewis and Clark (Montana), 1908 (later given to the State of Montana)
- Tumacacori, 1908
- Wheeler (Colorado), 1908 (given to the forest service in 1950)
- Mount Olympus, 1909 (now Olympic National Park)

Roosevelt also established Chalmette Monument and Grounds in 1907, the site of much of the Battle of New Orleans. It is now a part of Jean Lafitte National Historical Park and Preserve.

Chapter 8

REMEMBERING (AND RETRACING) THE CAMPING TRIP TODAY

Visiting Yosemite today in search of clues, reminders and evidence of that fabled 1903 camping trip is a project in itself. When I began researching this book last year, I found this announcement in the March 2012 edition of the "Yosemite Nature Notes" blog: "The park has a new official place name: Roosevelt Point. This is on the south rim of Yosemite Valley, just west of Sentinel Dome, near the top of Sentinel Falls. Some scholars believe that Muir and Roosevelt camped near here on the second night of their 1903 trip together. They're usually described as having camped at Glacier Point because that's a better known landmark than the forest near Sentinel Dome, and because of the famous photo-portrait of the two men at Glacier Point. Sentinel Creek would've been the most reliable water source for a camp, so it's likely that they actually spent the night there."

How wonderful, I thought. Somebody really remembered. Some more research produced the original proposal that had been submitted. This is part of it. As Judge William Alsup wrote in his "Justification for Selection of the Proposed Feature":

> *Of the two sitting Presidents known to have visited Yosemite (Theodore Roosevelt in 1903 and John F. Kennedy in 1962), Theodore Roosevelt was the only sitting president to camp in the Yosemite wilderness, and further, to have personally invited John Muir to this camp in the wilderness and in a snowfall. Roosevelt's exploration of Yosemite was not just a visit*

but was one of the most formative events in the Conservation Movement generally and in Yosemite history specifically.

The proposed feature was selected because its location is the only unnamed cape along the south rim in close proximity to the location of the snowfall camp, which was somewhere in the neighborhood of Sentinel Dome and, due to the need to camp near water, was very likely close to Sentinel Creek. While we cannot pin down the exact location of the Roosevelt-Muir snowfall camp, we know that it was near the proposed point.

I have made more than one hundred backcountry explorations in the Sierra since 1973 and fully endorse your concept of wilderness and leaving it be, including respecting its solitude even on our maps. We should not infringe on this policy without a compelling need. There is, however, a compelling need to remember Teddy Roosevelt and his historic outing in the Yosemite wilderness, an outing with none other than John Muir where they camped three nights, once in a snowstorm close by the proposed point in May 1903. That outing was followed in 1906 by the recession of Yosemite Valley to the United States to be made part of Yosemite National Park. The proposed Roosevelt Point is the only unnamed prominent picturesque point on that side of the Yosemite rim and happens to be in close proximity to their snow-bound camp in May 1903. This historic event deserves to be remembered on our maps as an ever-present reminder of the Roosevelt-Muir collaborations and of the importance of Teddy Roosevelt to Yosemite. No other place in Yosemite is named for Teddy Roosevelt (whereas Admiral Dewey and President Taft, oddly, are so remembered).

For the honorable Judge William Alsup, who spearheaded this project, it started back in about 1973, when he started hiking in the Sierras. Since that time, he has embarked on almost 150 backcountry trips in and around the Yosemite Valley. He loves the history of the Sierras so much that he has even written a pair of books, one about the 1864 expedition of the California geological survey and another entitled *Missing in the Minarets: The Search for Walter A. Starr Jr.*

Back in the 1980s, Alsup became friendly with a gentleman named Steve Medley, a lawyer who eventually gave up his legal career to dedicate his life to Yosemite as the president of the Yosemite Association, a nonprofit organization of eleven thousand members that supports the National Park Service.

Once Judge Alsup joined the board of the group, its members became friendly and would occasionally go on hikes and camp together. As the judge described to me, Medley was a wealth of information when it came to the area, and one evening ten or so years ago, he brought up a story about the 1903 Roosevelt camping trip. The tale occupied most of the conversation that evening, and these two men and another friend who was along began wondering why there wasn't any place named for Roosevelt in the park. After all, Taft and Dewey both had their names attached to places, but neither had done what Roosevelt had.

Looking around their campground and realizing that they were within perhaps half a mile of where Muir and Roosevelt camped their second night back in 1903, they decided that it was the perfect place to be called Roosevelt Point. From there, Judge Alsup put together a proposal aided by his friend Medley. They submitted the proposal and heard nothing at first, but within a year or so, a pair of men from a state agency in Sacramento contacted Alsup to tell him that they were very excited and interested in his proposal.

At first, they weren't sure that Alsup had the location right, but after more careful examination, they realized that the proposed site for Roosevelt Point was indeed almost precisely where the men had been in 1903. Energized, in short order the Board of Geographic Names approved the proposal, much to Alsup's delight, as he explained to me.

Tragically, Medley was killed in a car accident in 2006. But his efforts live on today at Roosevelt Point. As Judge Alsup described to me, "It was very satisfying that this happened. But if Steve hadn't told us that story I never would've had the idea. I'm not someone who seeks promotion or anything like that, and I haven't told many friends about this project. But it's something I'm very passionate about, and again I thank my friend for bringing it to my attention." The world thanks both of you, sir.

With mounting frustration, I also tried to track down the sleek and elegant Pullman train care called the "Elysian" that carried Roosevelt to California. Thankfully, Bob Webber in the Pullman Library was able to provide the answer in an e-mail. I wish it were better news:

Private Cars—G/S—Acadian & Elysian
(Old Plan Drawing List—Plan 1671)
Elysian Sold to WP (Western Pacific) on 9/27/1920
Per Dunscomb (WP Locomotives Passenger Trains and Cars) car was sold to WP for $20,213. Became WP 02, then renumbered to WP 104 7/8/1927, retired 11/30/1942—replaced by car No. 106. In storage until 12/1945, from which time until 4/51 used as locker room at Stockton roundhouse. Scrapped 4/51. Car was 82' 11.5" long, weighed

Roosevelt's personal train car, the elegant "Elysian," made by Pullman. It was scrapped in the early 1950s.

150,700 pounds had 36-inch six-wheel trucks, steel underframe, 9 chairs in dining room, 3 in observation room, and 9 berths.

As you can see, after serving as a locker room at the Stockton (California) roundhouse, it was scrapped in April 1951. Just think of what a museum piece that would be today.

Before heading to Yosemite, I decided to visit the small town of Raymond, where Roosevelt's train parked for three days while he camped. Back then it was a tourist destination—the rail gateway to Yosemite. Today it's a quiet, peaceful spot on the map. Lynn Northrop, who owns and runs the Raymond Museum, is a wealth of information, especially when it comes to Roosevelt's visit. She pointed out exactly where the station had been where the president pulled up. Today it's a large patch of grass. There's a house where the Bowen Hotel used to be, where Teddy spoke, but at least a piece of the original train track still remains in town.

Heading into Yosemite National Park, a good place to retrace some the footsteps of Roosevelt and Muir is at the Mariposa Grove of Giant Sequoias. This is where Roosevelt and his group first came to visit after having lunch at the Wawona Hotel. A two-mile trail leads past a variety of

The site where the Raymond train station once stood.

the famous cinnamon-colored giant trees, including the Grizzly Giant, next to which Roosevelt and company were photographed. The Wawona tunnel tree, which Roosevelt was driven through, fell to the ground in 1969 but still remains in place. The grove is also where Roosevelt and Muir spent the first night of their camping trip (as of this writing, the grove is under repair and will reopen in 2017).

A hike or a drive to Glacier Point allows one to marvel at the same views the men enjoyed upon awakening after night two of their camping trip, near the area today known as Roosevelt Point, overlooking the Yosemite Valley. It is breathtaking. I discovered that an image taken of Roosevelt that morning (along with the famous shots of Muir and Roosevelt posing together) that's always identified as being shot at Glacier Point was actually taken at Washburn Point, about a mile away.

Heading down to the valley, where their third night was spent, a sign marks the approximate site of the campground near Bridalveil Fall. The Jorgenson Cabin, where Roosevelt was to have spent a night but ended up camping another night, has been relocated to its present spot at the Pioneer Yosemite History Center.

Above: The site of the Bowen Hotel today.

Below: The last piece of original railroad track left in Raymond, California. The president's train would've rolled over these when he arrived to begin his adventure in Yosemite.

SOUTHERN PACIFIC RAILROAD
1886 - 1946
ORIGINAL TIES

Theodore Roosevelt and his distinguished party before the Grizzly Giant tree. *From left to right*: California governor George Pardee, Roosevelt, Presley N. Rixie, John Muir, Nicholas Butler, William Loeb and Benjamin Wheeler.

This wonderful complex includes many interesting old structures, stagecoaches and more, including the Jorgensen Cabin, which was the only structure Roosevelt spent time in during his camping trip with Muir (he took a brief tour of it). And it's located just a few minutes' walk from the historic Wawona Hotel, where Roosevelt began and ended his Yosemite Valley experience. The charming and peaceful establishment, a complex of old structures, dates back to the 1880s, and while Roosevelt didn't sleep here, he did eat lunch here (with Muir) and gave a speech just before heading back to Raymond to reboard his train and continue his trip. He did not eat in what is the dining room today but rather the room just adjacent to it.

Also on the Wawona Hotel property is the former studio of the famed artist Thomas Hill, whose paintings of Yosemite Valley and its environs are some of the most cherished on earth. As the Yosemite Conservancy described it, "A contributing structure to the National Historic Landmark status of the Wawona Hotel complex, the Thomas Hill Studio houses the Wawona Visitor Center. Here, the public can obtain information and wilderness permits; purchase maps, books and souvenirs; and become acquainted

The Grizzly Giant tree at Mariposa Grove today at the exact spot where Roosevelt and his group posed.

The Wawona Tunnel Tree that Roosevelt's group drove through in 1903. It collapsed in 1969 but still attracts visitors.

ON THIS SITE PRESIDENT THEODORE ROOSEVELT SAT BESIDE A CAMPFIRE WITH JOHN MUIR ON MAY 17, 1903 AND TALKED FOREST GOOD. MUIR URGED THE PRESIDENT TO WORK FOR PRESERVATION OF PRICELESS REMNANTS OF AMERICA'S WILDERNESS. AT THIS SPOT ONE OF OUR COUNTRY'S FOREMOST CONSERVATIONISTS RECEIVED GREAT INSPIRATION.

Above: The view from Glacier Point today, at the approximate spot where Roosevelt and Muir posed in 1903.

Right: Today, a sign marks the spot where Roosevelt and Muir spent their last night camping together near Bridalveil Fall at Yosemite.

The cabin of artist Chris Jorgensen, which Roosevelt visited while in Yosemite. It is now located near the Wawona Hotel as part of a museum.

with the contributions made by landscape artist Thomas Hill in protecting Yosemite and the big trees. The beautiful Douglas fir floors of the studio, which was originally constructed by Hill in 1884, must be refurbished and preserved to continue to welcome guests in the decades to come.

There is more information about that painting, as alluded to earlier. There are several accounts of Roosevelt entering this building that is still there today and leaving with this beautiful painting—presumably with staffers packing it aboard the train back to Washington, D.C. One example is this National Park Service notation: "During this visit, Roosevelt met Thomas Hill at his studio. Hill gave Roosevelt a painting of Bridalveil Fall that he had admired, and it returned with him to the White House." I located the beautiful painting in the White House's online archive, and it is indeed magnificent, featuring a sweeping view of the valley with a small man in the foreground, presumably to add some perspective. I also found a letter from Roosevelt to Hill thanking him for the gift, from July 6, 1903, and marked "personal":

Above: Today, Thomas Hill's studio still stands, serving as the visitors' center for the National Park Service next to the Wawona Hotel. It was here where Roosevelt paid the painter a visit before getting back on his train, as well as where Hill presented Roosevelt with a special gift: the painting he admired of Bridalveil Fall.

Opposite, top: The Wawona Hotel as it looks today.

Opposite, bottom: The only known photograph of the Roosevelt at Thomas Hill's studio near the Wawona Hotel. Here he is seen with Hill's wife, Willeta Hill (at left), with Estella Washburn in the middle.

My dear Mr. Hill:

I thank you very much for your kindness and appreciate you are having sent me the picture. I am glad you have devoted yourself to the assembly work. Surely nowhere is there greater chance for artists who love nature. With renewed thanks, sincerely yours

Theodore Roosevelt

The painting that Thomas Hill sent to Roosevelt after their meeting. As research for this book appears to prove, that tiny figure in the foreground is actually Theodore Roosevelt, added in by Hill after the two men met.

Note that Roosevelt says, "having sent me the picture." But something is wrong. This conflicts with the idea of the president's team taking the picture back with them from their visit. So I dug deeper into the story and found, buried in the May 19, 1903 edition of the long-gone *San Francisco Call* newspaper, this single reporter's note: "Mr. Hill proposed to paint the president in the foreground, just where he camped, and then send the canvas to Washington."

I went back and looked at the painting closer. Using a higher-resolution image, I enlarged the portion that includes the small figure in the foreground. While not the most faithful image of such an iconic figure as Roosevelt, it certainly appears to be him. Thus the clue in the letter seems to be answered. The painting did not leave that day. The painter, paying tribute to the president, made him part of the scenery.

Outside of that obscure and forgotten article, I do not believe that this has ever been publicly documented before. But now you know. As of this writing, I am in the process of making a case to the White House that the painting be placed in the Roosevelt Room. I will keep you posted.

Just as a final postscript, for anyone interested in the badger. Josiah became Archie Roosevelt's pet. When the animal got bigger, he found a new home at the Bronx Zoo in New York City. He lived there for many years and was visited there several times by the Roosevelt family.

INDEX